CRAIGINCHES

CRAIGINCHES
LIFE IN ABERDEEN'S PRISON

BRYAN GLENNIE
WITH SCOTT BURNS

BLACK & WHITE PUBLISHING

First published 2017
by Black & White Publishing Ltd
29 Ocean Drive, Edinburgh EH6 6JL

1 3 5 7 9 10 8 6 4 2   17 18 19 20

ISBN: 978 1 78530 121 6

A CIP catalogue record for this book is available from the British Library.

Typeset by Iolaire, Newtonmore
Printed and bound by CPI Group (UK) Ltd, Croydon, CR0 4YY

CONTENTS

Foreword By Sir Alex Ferguson, CBE

It was my privilege to know Bryan Glennie when I was manager at Aberdeen Football Club. We had a very close friendship and I spent a lot of time with his family.

At that time Bryan was working at the Craiginches Prison. His was one of the most intense experiences one can imagine. When listening to some of the events told by Bryan in graphic detail it made me wonder how the wardens got through each day.

As Bryan says himself, it is a life's education. Having to treat everyone differently, as their personalities could be miles apart, was a challenge that he thrived on.

I will always remember our trips to the Cup Finals at Hampden Park when Bryan and his family would come to my mother-in-law's house for their lunch before descending on the national stadium, which was only a couple of miles away.

On reading this book I think the reader will see a very interesting experience of life in an institution where all the officers have to be diligent, smart and aware of just how precarious the situation is in that profession. I think we owe Bryan and his colleagues a debt of thanks.

Sir Alex Ferguson, CBE

INTRODUCTION

I would like to thank you very much for taking the time to pick up my book.

My name is Bryan Edwin Glennie and I was a prison officer with the Scottish Prison Service for twenty-four years. The majority of my time was served at Her Majesty's Prison Aberdeen, or Craiginches as it was more commonly known in the North-east. HMP Aberdeen served the Granite City for 123 years before the gates were closed and locked for the final time in 2014. The prison has since been demolished and Craiginches is now nothing more than a not-so-distant memory.

HMP Aberdeen may have gone but for me, and so many others who worked there, it will never be forgotten. It was much more than a holding facility for prisoners. There was too much achieved inside and outside of those prison walls to simply be discarded or condemned to the vaults of Scotland's prison history. That was the main reason I decided to write this book.

My time at Craiginches was influential in my life, not just through my primary role as a prison officer but also through all the work, projects and monies the prison and the Community

Links Committee raised for a string of good causes across the North-east of Scotland.

All the staff went out with the simple aim of trying to raise the profile of Craiginches to the highest level possible and to make the prison the best it could be. So much so that our work led the Scottish Prison Service's former deputy director, Mr Alan Walker, to call it the 'jewel in the crown of the SPS'. I would also hope that most of the prisoners took something positive out of their time at Craiginches. Okay, it won't go down as the best period in their lives but it was our aim that they would leave with tools and skills for a positive future.

Many of the inmates got involved in some worthwhile projects and gave a lot back to the local communities. Much of that is never seen and all the prisoners should be commended for their part in Craiginches' success. As with most things at Craiginches, it was a real team effort. So if anyone was to say crime didn't pay around Craiginches then I would point to what we did at HMP Aberdeen and strongly disagree.

I enjoyed just about every minute of my twenty-four years at Craiginches. Every day was an adventure and more often than not my work gave me a real sense of achievement. It is a time I look back on with great pride.

That is why I would like to dedicate this book to all the staff, prisoners and volunteers who worked hard to make sure HMP Aberdeen will be remembered for all the right reasons. I would have been unable to complete it and make it a factual story without the help of all the individuals named and pictured in the book. I did my best to make contact with as many people as possible but it proved a very difficult task and if I have failed to get in touch with anyone named in the book then I do apologise.

I would also like to thank my co-author Scott Burns for his

vision in persuading me to put my thoughts and memories down into words and also for all the work he did in getting my book into print.

I would like to say a big thank you to Sir Alex Ferguson. He has been a good friend for many years and I would just like to thank the great man for agreeing to take time out of his busy schedule to do the foreword.

I would also like to show my appreciation to Black & White Publishing for having the faith to take my story and to make my book reality. They have produced a top quality book and been a big help every step of the way.

I have to say thank you to my good friend and lawyer George Mathers for his assistance and getting the book signed off, and to the Scottish Prison Service for granting their approval.

I would just like to finish off by saying that I hope you enjoy reading this book as much as I did writing it and I hope you, like myself, can look back on HMP Aberdeen and everything that was done and achieved there with great pride.

Bryan Glennie

ACKNOWLEDGEMENTS
FROM CO-AUTHOR SCOTT BURNS

I came to know Bryan Glennie as two of his grandchildren went to primary school, Fishermoss in Portlethen, with my oldest son, Ross. Through their seven years there I got to know Bryan and the Glennie family quite well.

On those early mornings we would initially exchange a quick wave or a hello but as the years progressed we would stop and have a quick chat about what was going on.

Bryan always had a wee story and a lot of these would come from his time as a prison officer at Craiginches.

More and more stories came to the fore and I thought to myself, Bryan has lived some life and must have a really good tales to tell.

I did often think to myself why doesn't Bryan consider writing a book?

I ran the idea past Bryan and we agreed to sit down one morning – after the school run, obviously – to have a discussion about a book and what stories he had to tell.

I sat with Bryan for a couple of hours as he rolled off a string of tales sprinkled with more than a fair share of big names thrown in for good measure.

I was in no doubt that Bryan's story had a book in it. I was more than happy to help him and give him a few hints and tips and a bit of guidance along the way.

Bryan then asked me if I would write the book for him. I had to think long and hard about that as Mrs Burns had already said I had too much on my plate.

Then I thought if I don't write it then Bryan's story may never find its way into print and that would have been a travesty in itself.

The biggest thing was trying to find time in my diary, and then when I did, trying to get Bryan in.

In typical Bryan style he would be out for his daily walk, keeping fit, or helping others, doing things like bowling coaching or the cycling proficiency at Fishermoss Primary School.

He may have retired but he is probably still as busy as ever and if he is not doing things with his family then he is helping others. That is the sort of person he is.

Bryan, you really are one of a kind and I hope my words can do your story justice.

I would also like to say thank you to Black & White Publishing for putting another book I have been involved with into print.

Also thank you to my wife, Amanda, and the boys, Ross and Aaron. I might have some time to see you now!

Scott Burns

PS: Thank you for the golf balls, Bryan. I think half of them are mine anyway from my wayward tee shots from the tenth hole at Portlethen Golf Club.

1

CRAIGINCHES IS BORN

The first known 'official' prison in Aberdeen dates back to 1394, when the Tolbooth Prison and Courthouse were sanctioned and proposed for the city's Castle Street.

It was claimed at the time of its building that it was more of a holding facility than a prison. Prisoners were held there until their fate was decided – which could be anything from imprisonment, if they were lucky, to slow torture or death in more extreme circumstances. It could certainly be classed as barbaric.

Not surprisingly, tales from the Tolbooth were enough to strike fear into the hearts of the majority of Aberdonians and natives of the north-east of Scotland, although, as always, there were others who, no matter what, couldn't keep themselves on the right side of the law.

The Tolbooth was stated as the only penal institution in Aberdeen until around 1636 when the House of Correction was built and came into operation.

It pretty much did what it said on the tin – a house of correction, trying to reform characters and to get them back on the right side of the law. It was the first of its kind in Scotland and was the brainwave of the City Provost, Alexander Jaffray, who had taken office just twelve months earlier.

He had made it one of his main aims to try and clean up Aberdeen city centre by removing from the streets vagabonds, beggars, stray children, delinquents and others, who today would be classed as undesirable. The House of Correction was run in line with the beliefs of the Church. It aimed to get individuals back on the straight and narrow and to get them living their lives the right way. The House provided lodgings and food in exchange for work in the clothing and textile industry. It certainly gave people hope and the opportunity to escape from an otherwise sad existence. The House of Correction continued to play its part and it was certainly a far different proposition from the Tolbooth, which catered for the more hardened of criminals.

Aberdeen was nicknamed the Granite City for the number of houses, offices and apartments that were constructed out of the clean, grey and imposing stone. It could also have been used to describe the growing underbelly of crime in Aberdeen during those early years and it quickly became clear that times were a changing and there was a need for another prison to compliment the Tolbooth.

The Bridewell Prison, or West Prison, as it was also known, was built to meet that particular demand. It was located at the north end of the city centre in Rose Street. It served as the city's second prison and took some of the strain off the Tolbooth, which was bursting at the seams – so much so that there was a need for the Tolbooth itself, to eventually be replaced and upgraded.

A new Tolbooth facility was built in 1819 behind the original building. It was no less forgiving and in time eventually became known as the East Prison, due to its location at the heart of Aberdeen's city centre.

The new Tolbooth remained as the main prison for more

than half a century before it was confirmed in the late 1870s that it had served its time and Aberdeen was to get a new prison.

The authorities were basically left with no option and were pushed into the move to replace the rather dated and inadequate East and Bridewell Prisons. There were particular concerns over the East Prison, which failed its final inspection set out by the 1877 Prison Act. The East Prison was basically condemned, which was a fair achievement as the standards back then weren't as high as they are today. The problem was that it couldn't be put out of commission until an alternative had been found and built!

There was also limited land within the city of Aberdeen so the authorities had to widen their horizons and look outwith the city for a suitable solution. It still needed to be somewhere close enough to the city centre courts and jails to allow the prisoners to be easily and safely transported to and from the new facility.

Her Majesty's Prison commissioners considered several options in and around the city before they settled on a site in nearby Torry, adjacent to the Wellington Bridge.

Torry, a former Royal Burgh, is famed for housing the families of fishermen in and around the north-east port. It officially became part of Aberdeen when the boundaries were pushed across the River Dee to satisfy the increasing population.

The 10-acre site pinpointed by the HM Prison commissioners belonged to the Aberdeen Land Association. They were prepared to sell if the price was right. A deal was quickly struck and the news made local headlines. The *Aberdeen Journal* newspaper, on 13th September 1889, greeted the story with the heading: 'New prison for Aberdeen'.

The same article also explained why the new facility was

so desperately needed due to the fact that the East Prison had fallen into such disrepair.

It read: 'The need for a new prison has, as is pretty well-known, long since been recognised. In many respects the present structure is wholly inadequate for the necessity of a large district with which it is connected, not only from the point of accommodation but also in terms of the sanitary and other basic requirements.' The initial costs for the Torry-based prison were budgeted at around £20,000 – a massive sum at that time. The new Aberdeen prison quickly began to rise out of the Torry skyline as it took shape. It was visible from Aberdeen's city centre, as it stood on the south side of the River Dee, a giant bastion and deterrent against the criminal underbelly.

The *Aberdeen Journal* wrote: 'The existing prison in Lodge Walk is hid in a corner, as it were, while the new jail is set on a hill as a warning to evil doers.' It added: 'The old prison was a prison but the new prison is a palace. It is hoped that with its perfect sanitation and its adaptability to modern requirements, it will be even more powerful than the old institution in deterring from crime and in reclaiming criminals.'

The progress and build of the prison was quick and the *Aberdeen Journal* continued to keep the North-east public up to speed with its rapid progress.

It stated: 'Her Majesty's Prison at Craiginches is nearing completion, standing as it does on an eminence overlooking the silvery Dee, it is an imposing and pleasing feature in the landscape, though its presence must serve as a reminder that the criminal classes are still with us.

'The plans were prepared under the supervision of Her Majesty's Commissioner for Prisons in Scotland and under the personal direction of Colonel McHardy. He has a great experience in building such institutions and all the best

4

modern improvements have been introduced to ensure the new prison will be an ideal edifice.

'The total cost will be around £20,000. The sole contract was placed in the hands of Messers D. McAndrew and Co. in September 1889 and is expected to be completed by 31st May 1891. Progress has already been made and fully warrants the expectation that it will be completed easily within that timescale.

'It is hoped the genial Governor Mr Rutledge, who has for many years managed the old prison so admirably, will be spared to preside over the destinies of the newer and much more conveniently arranged prison.' The *Aberdeen Journal* got its wish as Mr Routledge was put in charge when 'Craiginches' or HMP Aberdeen, finally opened its giant wooden gates for the first time at the start of the 1890s, at a slightly more inflated cost of £36,000. Craiginches came just two years after a similar and slightly larger prison had been opened further up the north-east coast in the fishing town of Peterhead, or the 'Blue Toon' as it is more affectionately nicknamed.

HMP Aberdeen originally housed around 155 inmates and at the time was seen as state of the art. It was something different and much more progressive than its predecessors. It may have been described as a palace compared to what had come before but there was one thing for certain: the prisoners were certainly never going to be treated like royalty.

Some of the first recorded prisoners included an infamous drunk simply called 'Toughie', (George Thomson) a city blacksmith who was sentenced to fifteen years for committing various assaults against his daughter between 1883 and 1891.

'Toughie' spent most of his life intoxicated and that was at the heart of his problems. He was known in and around Aberdeen for all the wrong reasons. A report from the

Aberdeen Journal which was later reproduced in the *Press and Journal* basically summed up 'Toughie.'

The reproduced extract read: 'A newspaper report of Toughie's umpteenth appearance in court could have been scripted by the Monty Python team. The accused rattled into the dock in double time and doffing his battered "brown", smoothed his hair and listened attentively to the complaint.'

After the clerk had finished, Toughie, in a pleading voice, said: 'I wish to adjourn my case to Saturday.' That request led the rest of the court to burst into fits of laughter. Order was restored and the clerk's response was: 'You must plead guilty or not guilty.' Toughie said: 'I plead guilty.' So the clerk told him: 'Well, you do not require an adjournment.' Quick as a flash the accused's response was: 'If you please, I do not feel well and that is the reason.' Once again the roars of laughter could be heard round the court. The magistrate himself had clearly had enough by this point and said: 'Really, there is no use waiting until Saturday.' Toughie was not one to give up without a fight. He went on to have the last laugh when he said: 'Oh, yes, I might be better on Saturday and you might be more obliging.' The magistrate wasn't and Toughie was sent down to become one of the first prisoners through the gates at Craiginches.

The transportation of those initial prisoners to HMP Aberdeen was also documented in the *Aberdeen Journal* newspaper on 10th June 1891.

Its published article stated: 'Yesterday morning the prisoners in the old county jail were removed to the new prison at Craiginches. Arrangements had been made for their quiet removal and that was affected speedily and without any hitches. The "flitting" took place at three o'clock, the prisoners being conveyed to their new quarters in a bus with blinded windows, and on which the prison warders mounted guard.

'Mr Rutledge, the governor, supervised the operations and a small force of police officers were also on duty, under Inspector Forbes and Sergeant Simpson. The prisoners, who numbered in all forty-three, seemed to look upon the change as an agreeable break in prison life.'

And so life in Craiginches began.

2

Postal Strike Sends Me to Jail

The infamous United Kingdom postal workers strike of 1971 was the catalyst for a major change in my career and my life. Up to that point I had been a postman in my home village of Insch in Aberdeenshire.

The strike came to the fore over the pay and conditions of Post Office staff. The money its workers got was below the average living wage and after months and months of failed negotiations the union and the workers felt they had no choice but to go out on strike.

It turned quite hostile and there seemed to be no short-to-medium-term resolution on the horizon. The strike went on for weeks. It also meant I and my fellow postmen didn't receive a penny in wages while the majority of the United Kingdom was left waiting for their mail, which quickly began to pile up.

We had to survive on handouts from the union but even then it was only a fraction of the same wages that had forced us to strike in the first place. I had to try and make ends meet by doing odd jobs in and around Insch. I had a family to support, I had two young daughters, Jacqueline and Lesley, and it was a really difficult time. In the end,

I felt I'd had my fill of the strike and the Post Office and I decided I needed to get another job. I just couldn't see a way forward – the strike had left me completely sickened and out of pocket.

I considered various career changes but I had my heart set on joining the Scottish Prison Service. It was the logical choice for me as I had already been working in the civil service. I had eleven and a half years' service with the Post Office which I knew was completely transferable – my service and my pension. I had done my research and joining the prison service made the most sense. I have to say I didn't really consider any other careers because I wanted to go fully down the road of the prison service to see if I could make that dream a reality. If that didn't happen then I would have had to look elsewhere but the prison service was always going to be my first port of call.

The good thing was that the Scottish Prison Service was also on something of a recruitment drive at that time. They were advertising for staff and I knew it was pretty much now or never.

I had thought a lot about the financial side and stability of joining but a big thing was also my career as well. I was ambitious and I saw the prison service as a big challenge to me. It was something completely different to what I had faced up to then in my life. I had a background in sport. I also had a number of other additional qualifications which I felt I could put to full use in the prison sector. Those aspects were hugely appealing to me. I just hoped I would be as appealing to the SPS.

There were a few negatives to the job. Prison work can be dangerous. At times you could be at risk, and then there was the change in shift patterns. Up until then, after I had posted my last letter of the day I knew I had the rest of the day to myself. If I got into the SPS I would have different shifts and would also have to work weekends. However, for me the positives far outweighed the minor negatives. It was and remained an easy decision.

The recommendation from Dougie Ruxton also gave me an insight into what I could expect. He was a prison officer at HMP Aberdeen. His wife, Isma, was at school with me and her parents still lived in Insch at that time. They used to come out to visit her parents. I knew her parents well, being the local postman.

Dougie was also an Insch boy (or loon). He was older than me and I had known him for most of my life. He used to play for Insch's football team in the Donside League earlier in his career before joining the prison service.

I was just a teenager at that point. I was still too young to play but I liked to be involved and became the unofficial kit-man (or boy!). Granny Gibson used to wash the football strips for the team. She used to stay beside me in Church Terrace in the village. So I used to pick up the big brown case of strips after she had washed and ironed them. I would then carry them to wherever the team was due to play, whether it be Kemnay, Kennethmont or Keig on a Tuesday or a Thursday night.

I loved to go on my travels with the team, although it was a slightly easier job when they were playing at home. I used to put out all the strips in the changing room and then collect all the gear again after the game. I would then take it all back to Granny Gibson, where the whole process would start again for the next match. Dougie was a good player and I knew him from my adventures with Insch FC, while his family was also well known in the village because his dad had been a well-respected banker. They were a very prominent family within the community.

So I went and asked Dougie's parents-in-law if they could get Dougie to give me a shout the next time he was in Insch. I explained to them how I was thinking about joining the prison service. They were as good as gold and sure enough Dougie came round and chapped on my door. I invited him in and we had a cup of tea and I explained my situation with the Post Office and how I felt it was time for a change in direction.

Dougie also thought the prison service would be an ideal career path for me to pursue. He understood my reasons for wanting to join and he was also very balanced and told me about things on the other side of the coin, which weren't as appealing.

Also if I was lucky enough to get a position at HMP Aberdeen then it would mean longer journeys into work, driving the twenty-seven miles from Insch to the Granite City. For me, it was a small price to pay. It was what I had always wanted to do and my mantra has always been: 'You don't know until you have tried it.'

Dougie then turned to me and said: 'I think you should have a go because you would like it and I am more than happy to recommend it to you.' So I went and got the application forms, filled them in, sent them off and kept my fingers crossed.

I then got a letter inviting me for a medical. There were five people there that day but only my future colleague, Walter Noble, and I were successful.

We were then interviewed by senior staff and had a medical. At that point, we were told there would be no guarantees and even if we were successful then we might not get stationed at HMP Aberdeen. We could have been sent to any of Scotland's prisons. That was the one wee negative but if that had happened then I would have just got on with it. I would have lived in digs until I could get the family sorted out. Dougie had warned me of this possibility during our chat but he'd also told me that the prison service had accommodation and put officers and their families up if they had to move further afield.

I then got a letter that confirmed that I had been a successful candidate and they wanted to offer me a job. On top of that was the added bonus that I was going to be stationed at HMP Aberdeen. That was a huge relief. I was still at the Post Office but, ironically, the strike had been resolved and I was back on the front line with much better terms and conditions. I have to say even those improved benefits were never going to change my mind. The prison service was where I wanted to go and I was finally getting my chance. I was absolutely delighted.

I had basically five weeks from getting the letter to my starting date. It was a bit of a whirlwind. It became more and more exciting and appealing as every day passed. I remember when I made that trip to HMP Aberdeen for the first time. I was like a kid on his way to school for the first time – not knowing what lay ahead.

We were given a guided tour, shown the different jobs and then placed on our shift. It was as simple as that. The new starts were broken in gently with day shifts just until we got settled in and to give us time to find our feet.

There were two divisions or shifts at that point and I was allocated to the second division. That was also the same division as Dougie Ruxton. It was good seeing a friendly face. It is quite funny, looking back, because half of that team was made up of boys like Dougie and myself who were from out in the country, from Aberdeenshire or beyond, and the other half was comprised of men from the city. I think that was a major reason there was such good harmony in the second division. We were all similar people with pretty close mindsets. Another member of our team was Scott Ogilvie, who went on to become a future governor of Craiginches and a boss of mine.

Walter Noble was a fellow officer. He started with the prison service at the same time as me but I got three days more holidays than him because of my continued service from the Post Office. My previous guise also helped me in terms of pay. I got a little more pay than the other new recruits because of my combined service.

I worked nearly four months in the prison before I went down to the training college at Polmont, where I did twelve weeks alongside Walter.

It was a course to prepare you for life in the prison service. We were introduced to the rules and regulations and the standards required from ourselves. It was and still is basically a school for the prison service. The tutors got us ready for when we went back to our posts. It covered just about everything, even drug abuse, which I would have to say was never very prominent back in the early 1970s within the prison walls. There was also a lot of physical and sporting work, along with marching. It was hard work but enjoyable.

I was even lucky enough to win the Baton of Honour at the training college. The Baton of Honour went to the top student on the course – it was the first time anyone from Aberdeen had won it. Now it was time to put my theory into practice.

3

The Changing Face of Craiginches

Recently, on a bus, I overheard one woman say to another that so-and-so had been sent to prison and that it was terrible there. I am afraid that she, like many more, was under the impression that Craiginches was some sort of concentration camp where prisoners were overworked and subject to brutal conditions. May I be allowed a wee space in your columns to correct these false impressions? I have had a taste of it, so I should know.

The original entrance to Her Majesty's Prison Aberdeen, as you would expect, had a really imposing presence. The outside gates were made of tough English oak. You would go through those gates and be met with the gatehouse and then a second set of iron gates. Any visitors, for safety and security reasons, would then have to wait for the wooden gates to be closed before the metal gates were opened to the inner sanctum of the prison.

You entered the main gate area, where the governor's office was situated, along with the gate office, staff muster area and the officers' staffroom. On the other side next to the governor's office was a waiting room and visiting area.

The original main building, which was constructed in 1891, remained intact and central throughout the life of Craiginches.

The prison was broken into two main halls – A and B.

The A Hall housed mainly locally convicted prisoners over its three galleries or levels. They also held a number of prisoners who were serving sentences of eighteen months or more.

B Hall also had three galleries. It housed untried adults, males under twenty-one and convicted young offenders until they were transferred to the Young Offenders Institution at Polmont. Those over twenty-one were kept mainly on the second floor, while the others remained on the other levels.

Both halls were modernised through time as were various other aspects of the prison, as they had to adapt to an ever-changing outside world.

One of the main issues and talking points of British prison life has been slopping out. Craiginches was an old Victorian period prison that didn't always have internal sanitation and toilets for each cell so the inmates had no option but to slop out. That was the way it was and the prisoners just had to get on with it.

Each prisoner was given a pot with a lid on it which they had to use for the toilet when they were locked up in their cells. The prisoners would come out every morning to the public urinal and empty and clean their pots. There they would find all the disinfectants, cleaners and brushes that were needed to clean the pots.

When the £1 million sanitation project was brought into Craiginches in the 1980s that was definitely a major step forward, although I would say that it was probably too late in coming. They did all the work to modernise the prison yet a few decades later it was flattened to rubble. I think what counted against Craiginches and the old Peterhead prison was that they were so old. The buildings were tired and antiquated and there was very little else the Scottish Prison Service could do to prolong their lifespans.

Toilets and wash-hand basins were put into just about every cell. It was a major change. You have to remember when the prison was first built there were six large baths installed and that was seen as more than adequate for the inmates. Could you imagine that now?

You hear the people now say how slopping out is against people's human rights. Granted, it wasn't nice but it was a sign of the times and it was also a prison. You now hear all these former prisoners who are looking to try and sue because they felt their human rights had been impinged. That is a joke. A lot of these people are at it. They are just trying to play the system and looking to profit from it at the same time. They see it as an avenue they can latch on to and try to get free or easy money from. It is frustrating, especially as the money could be put to so many other different uses.

Another major project at Craiginches was to install something else that people outside of prison take for granted – simple heating.

Prior to heated cells the prisoners had to make do with extra blankets to get them through the long winter nights. It was pretty simplistic.

I remember when the authorities started the heating project. The installation was a major job. The biggest problem was getting it into every cell because the contractors basically had to drill through the thick walls to get the piping for the heating through. I remember that was a major headache because they were basically trying to drill holes through pure granite. A lot easier said than done. They were about two feet thick and when they first started their drills were hardly making a mark.

During each project, like the heating and sanitation, there

was major upheaval in the prison. Inmates had to be moved and temporarily rehoused while their allotted cell was worked on.

During that time we had to double up prisoners in some cells. That wasn't really common policy unless it was in the large communal cell, which was Number 1-18. That could easily hold five or six prisoners.

I know that when the prison was modernised with heating and sanitation the inmates saw it as a major step forward and both additions as great luxuries compared to what they had been used to in the past.

I remember I really felt we had moved into the twenty-first century when we had the electric gates installed at the prison entrance.

The new gatehouse still had two gates but it was a lot easier to open and close. I suppose it did make the prison that bit more secure, although to get through the gates you still had to go through the same process as before – opening one gate and closing it before you opened the inner gate. We also used to send an officer out whenever the gates were opened to check who and what was coming into the prison and then escort them through another inner gate and into the prison to wherever they were going.

The prison authorities also built an entire new front entrance at Craiginches. That included the new gatehouse, an office block, a Training for Freedom unit and a muster/staffroom, where we used to eat and have our breaks. The new complex also included the main office store and visiting room, and right at the bottom was the female unit. That was the part of the jail where we were able to keep untried female prisoners. Basically, that was an area for women who had been arrested and were waiting to go to court to be sentenced.

From 1974 Craiginches had its own stipulated female block.

It was located adjacent to the administration block. It was staffed by two female officers and five Temporary Female Assistants to cover the entire shift cycle. The wing also had a large day room with Sky television, a video and pool table.

Craiginches had various other facelifts. Around £250,000 was spent on a new gym and new kitchen facilities. The new cooking facilities were a godsend to the staff and made it easier to cater for such big numbers and also allowed them to open up their menus a lot more.

An education centre was also added. It was well used. Teachers would come in and offer a range of subjects to the prisoners, from art to English. They would get a lesson for an hour or so a week and then we would take them back to their cells. Quite a few prisoners went to those classes. They weren't as popular as the football or social events but the other problem for us was that we had to limit the numbers because of the size of the classrooms.

Like most remand halls in the penal system, staff in B Hall were required to incorporate management skills with a balanced measure of control, enforcement, good humour and compassion.

It didn't matter what was done, the basic problem was that the demand for prison cells in Aberdeen far outweighed what Craiginches could supply. That led to the prison's biggest problem – overcrowding.

Having too many prisoners was always a problem, especially in the latter years of HMP Aberdeen. It didn't help that Craiginches had to take inmates in from other areas of Scotland to a prison that was already bursting at the seams. The issue of overcrowding would always be flagged up during the Scottish Prisons Service's annual reports in the prison's later years.

I have to say it wasn't really as big an issue during my time at Craiginches – apart from the time when there were riots in Kincorth, a suburb in the south side of Aberdeen.

If memory serves me correctly, something had kicked off in a local pub. It escalated into a mass brawl before the police had to step in to defuse the situation. I believe their presence only added more fuel to proceedings and it ended with mass arrests. More than twenty male prisoners ended up being sent up to HMP Aberdeen. Those extra bodies ended up pushing B Hall very close to the edge.

There was also a limit to how many prisoners we could safely house. We eventually had to put some of our prisoners into A Hall to lessen the strain. They still had to be treated as untried prisoners even though they were in beside the more hardened inmates. It wasn't normal practice but we didn't have any other option. We were just relieved when the court reopened so we could get them transported across the city to face their charges and to help us bring some form of normality back into place.

The problem is that the changes were only ever short-term solutions and in time that was why the Scottish Prison Service had to look for alternatives.

DEATH ROW

4

THE LAST HANGING IN SCOTLAND

The 15th August 1963 might not be a date that is that well known when it comes to Scotland's history. Yet it is one that will be forever a landmark in the country's prison system. It was the day that the final hanging took place in Scotland and it was at Her Majesty's Prison Aberdeen. It is something that will ensure Craiginches is always remembered.

The final execution was of a prisoner called Henry 'Harry' John Burnett. He was sentenced to death at the age of just twenty-one for the murder of a merchant seaman called Thomas Guyan after they had got involved in a bizarre love triangle.

Burnett started seeing Guyan's wife, Margaret, after they had split. They had met while working together at John R. Stephen Fish Curers in Aberdeen. It led to the pair moving in together at Burnett's home in Skene Terrace. Burnett, however, still had long-term doubts at the back of his own mind. He had severe trust issues and became so insecure that when he left home it was reported he would leave Margaret locked in the house because he feared she would end up leaving him.

It was hardly a healthy relationship and not surprisingly

Margaret wasn't keen to stay put. She decided to leave Burnett to return to her husband, Guyan. She went back to Skene Terrace to collect her son, Keith, along with a family friend, Georgina Cattanagh, and told Burnett she was leaving him. Burnett went berserk and it was reported that he pulled out a knife and put it up at Margaret's throat before he pulled her back inside the house. Minutes later he stormed out of the house leaving both women shaken but unharmed.

Burnett went to see his brother, Frank, at his workplace to let him know what had happened. He was urged to go to the police but declined and instead headed to Frank's Bridge of Don home where he knew he kept a shotgun. Burnett burst the lock and the case, took the gun and cartridges, and jumped on a bus to Guyan's flat, where he forced his way in and shot him in the face. Burnett then stole a car from a petrol station but finally gave himself up after being pursued by a police car just outside of Ellon. He surrendered after Margaret agreed to marry him!

Things looked bleak for Burnett, as it was reported that his first words in the police interview room were: 'I gave him both barrels – he must be dead.' The case went to trial and Burnett's defence claimed that at the time of the crime their client was insane. However, they failed to convince the jury. It was widely predicted that Burnett would be found guilty and the expected sentence was to be life imprisonment. The case was lost but there was no leniency shown as Burnett was sentenced to death by hanging at Aberdeen High Court on 25th July 1963 after a short two-day trial.

The news sent shockwaves around the city, as it was the first hanging to take place in the Granite City. They had been commonplace in most other major cities in the United Kingdom but to the main fishing port in the North-east it was something of a culture shock.

Yet Burnett wasn't actually the first man to be sentenced to hanging in Aberdeen. On 1st February 1956 a prisoner named Robert James Boyle was also sentenced to the same fate. He was due to be hung on 10th March 1956. Special orders were even drawn up and executioner Stephen Wade was given the order but Boyle on appeal was given a late reprieve. His sentence was reduced to life imprisonment.

Burnett wasn't to be as fortunate. He returned to Craiginches, where he was held in the condemned cell while he awaited his fate. The cell was the prison's old B Hall until 1962, when the new condemned cell/execution chamber was built. It also included new workshops and an education unit.

There was no appeal from Burnett and at just before 8 a.m. on Thursday 15th August he was summoned to the newest gallows in Britain at that point. A prison officer confirmed Burnett was in a state of shock as he sat in his cell in his final few minutes and waited pensively for the call to make that final journey of his life. He was also offered a stimulant around 7.30 a.m.

The prisoner was said to have got on well with the prison guards and on his way he even identified to his escorts and prison officer the joints in the skirting board revealing the doors where he thought he would take his last steps to the hangman's noose.

Executioner Harry Allen, an Englishman, and his assistant Samuel Plant performed the execution, like they did for the majority of prison hangings between 1941 and 1964. He was the chief executioner at twenty-nine hangings and assisted at fifty-three others. Allen, who wore a bow tie as a mark of respect to his victims, had also performed the last execution in Northern Ireland when he hanged Robert McGladdery at Crumlin Road Prison in Belfast two years earlier. He was also involved in the second to last hanging in England at

Strangeways, where Gwynne Owen Evans died in 1964.

Allen's eye for detail ahead of his executions was notorious. He would take note of the prisoner's age, weight and height so he could calculate precisely how long the rope had to be to ensure a swift death.

The day of Burnett's execution was one that caused outrage outside of the prison. More than 200 people protested at Craiginches' gates to try and get the authorities to change their minds. That was always unlikely as Burnett's family, along with that of Guyan's, had already tried in vain to get a reprieve and their loved one's death sentence downgraded. It also left the prison service and authorities on edge. They had to double the staff they had on the gates, with protesters shouting 'Murderers!' and other forms of abuse to guards and staff behind the gates.

His former lover, Margaret Guyan, visited Burnett the day before his execution to say her farewells. He was also given all his clothing the night before, everything but his shirt and tie – for obvious reasons.

The layout of Craiginches meant that on the day of the hanging all the prisoners located in the east side of A Hall had to be moved, as their cells were adjacent to the condemned cell. This was so none of them could see the hangman or any of the witnesses to the death. The death schedule for that day ordered all prisoners to be locked up in their cells by 7.30 a.m. and they were scheduled to remain there until 9.30 a.m.

It wasn't until Allen and Plant had arrived to start their preparations that they realised there was a major issue. The drop platform and hooks on the roof had been put up facing the wrong way. By that time, it was too late to make alterations and Burnett had to be walked round on to the platform rather than straight on to it. His hands and feet were then bound and then the hangman placed the noose and hood in place and made his final preparations.

The sentence was witnessed by the prison governor, the chaplain, chief officer, engineer officer, a nurse and the two prison guards.

At just after 8 a.m. Burnett was declared dead as the watching magistrates witnessed his execution. The prison chaplain said a few words of prayer and by 8.05 a.m. the prison was ready to get back to normal service.

Burnett's body was then buried in an unmarked grave, which had been dug out the previous day within the prison walls. It was also normal practice for details of any execution to be put up on the door of the prison, but such was the ill-feeling around the prison that no notice was ever displayed.

By 10.30 a.m. all the prisoners were back at their work.

The Murder (Abolition of the Death Penalty) Act in 1965 then suspended the death penalty for the next five years. Campaigners finally got their wish when the death penalty was finally abolished in 1969. 'Judicial hanging' has never appeared on a death certificate in Scotland again.

Burnett had become infamous through his death. He was one of thirty-four people hanged in Scotland in the twentieth century. One hanging was carried out in Aberdeen and Inverness, three in Perth and the rest were shared between the capital, Edinburgh, and Glasgow.

Clearly, hangman Harry Allen knew the writing was on the wall for those in his profession. He was one of a dying breed. He told one of the prison officers that day at HMP Aberdeen he felt there would be a softening of the law and a move to imprisonment and away from the death sentence and capital punishment.

Burnett's family was given some closure when in 2014 they were allowed to exhume his body from the grounds

of Craiginches before it closed. The then Scottish government confirmed the move in a short statement, which read:
'The remains were recovered from the prison grounds and
a private ceremony was held at Aberdeen Crematorium on
August 7, 2014.'

5

Suicide Watch and Death

Suicide watch is common in prison life, especially amongst first-time inmates. It can be a real shock to their system. People don't know what to expect and I suspect that nothing can help you prepare for life inside – apart from maybe past stints inside. For some people it is a way of life going in and out of jail. For others it can feel like the end of the world.

Even now prisons have moved on. They are full of mod cons and the latest technology but when I started out at Craiginches it was a hundred thousand miles away from that. It was a massive Victorian building with no proper heating and no real sanitation with prisoners having to slop out. For many prisoners it can be too much and it was viewed as hell on earth.

When prisoners were admitted to HMP Aberdeen they would come into the reception and would have their details taken. They would then be checked out medically by the prison nurse. He would assess their physical and mental health and if he thought they were a risk to themselves then he would put them on suicide watch. This meant being housed on a wing of cells which were kept under constant supervision so individuals couldn't do any harm to themselves. Within a few days most of the prisoners got accustomed to their new surroundings and you could slowly break them in to the ways of prison life.

There were also other inmates who maybe felt down and had tried to take their lives after they had been inside for a period of time. It had maybe become too much for them.

It is bizarre because when I started work at Craiginches it would have been so easy for prisoners to take their own lives.

They used to get a fresh razor blade every Sunday for shaving purposes. That was long before the disposable razor. When the prisoners handed in their old blade they were given a new one for the next seven days. So if people wanted to self-harm they didn't have to look too far. Imagine prisoners being given open razor blades in prison today. Some prisons would be turned into bloodbaths!

DEATH

Death is also a harsh reality in prison. When inmates are sentenced to life then at times that is exactly what it can mean.

Prisoners can obviously die of natural causes but there have been times when they have taken their own lives. We had a handful of prisoners who committed suicide in my time at Craiginches. Most of the time prisoners had taken their bed sheets and hung themselves.

I remember one morning I had to open up. The senior officer was otherwise engaged and basically I had to do a head count to make sure the numbers from the previous night remained the same. That meant getting the prisoners up and out of their cells.

When I went to a well-known prisoner's cell I couldn't see him lying in bed so I opened the door to check and there he was lying on the floor. He was a really great guy and I just saw his bed unmade. He was lying on a blanket on the floor with one foot still up on the bed.

I went up to him and I knew right away he was stone dead. He had passed away during the night.

I immediately shouted to the other officers to get the prisoners back in their cells. Right away they knew something was wrong. I then had to call for the on-duty nurse. He came down and checked the prisoner and confirmed my worst fears that he had passed away.

These days you would probably get grief counselling to deal with situations like that. Back then you just had to put a brave face on it and get on with things.

It was just part of prison life, especially when you have so many inmates in for longer sentences or life.

The next of kin then had to be contacted and informed before the body was signed over to the authorities and taken to the mortuary. Then they went on for their final journey, whether that be a burial or cremation or whatever path they were going to take.

A Hall –

The Prison Wing

6

A Day in Craiginches

I will give you a bit of an insight into the daily process at HMP Aberdeen and to what a prisoner would have faced after they had been sent down to Craiginches.

The inmate would have been escorted from the court and transported across the city to the prison reception, where duty officers would have been waiting to do the paperwork and finalise the transfer into the care of the Scottish Prison Service.

The prisoner would then be taken through the reception and into a nearby room where they would be examined by the duty nurse. This was to make sure they were physically and mentally fit and well. After the new recruit was assessed, and if everything was okay, they would be assigned to a cell in A Hall, which housed our convicted criminals. The cell they were put in would depend on their crime or crimes and the length of sentence.

If the prisoner was in for a longer stretch, then they would be likely to be given a cell of their own, and if it was a so-called lesser sentence then they would go into a communal cell, which they might have to share with other inmates.

The morning opening up allowed the prisoners to go and

get washed, shaved and cleaned up. In the early days they would also have had to clean their toilet pots but that was no longer the case after slopping out became a thing of the past. Any prisoner who was on medication would also be administered this at that point.

At this stage, the prisoner could report to the officer-in-charge and request a meeting with the governor if they felt they had a personal matter or issue they wanted to discuss or talk about. The gallery officer would deal with more mundane requests like sorting out visiting orders or any letters that were to be sent out by a new arrival. Remember this was something new, especially for a prisoner who was in for the first time.

Beyond this point, the prisoner was pretty much submerged into everyday prison life. If there were any who were perhaps struggling to adjust or looked vulnerable, then we would keep a close eye on them – it was a massive culture shock for them, with the exception of maybe the more hardened criminals.

Craiginches, like every other institution within the Scottish Prison Service, was very regimented as to the structure of the day. That way everybody knew what they were doing and it added a bit of discipline to the lives of the occupants. At times that was all some people needed to get them back on an even keel.

Craiginches would be sprung into life by the guards going round the cells for the 6 a.m. wake-up and morning head count. Those prisoners who had special dietary requests would be sent through to the dining room to get their break-fast first. It was an early start and they would go around 7 a.m., pick up their breakfasts and return to their cells to eat it.

The morning menu would consist of options like porridge, toast, bread and butter, and either a portion of bacon, black pudding or sausage, along with a cup of tea.

After those inmates were fed and watered then the other prisoners would be taken through to the dining room. It certainly wasn't a leisurely breakfast. The inmates all had to be finished and ready to start their day jobs by 7.45 a.m., whether that was in the work sheds or elsewhere within the prison. This was also the point where we would take another head count to make sure none of the prisoners had sneaked off.

The prisoners would be hard at it until around 10 a.m. when tea was taken around the various work places to give everyone their mid-morning cuppa before it was back to the hard graft. If you were ill and had requested to see a doctor or the governor, then this would also happen around this point. If the medical staff decided, after your check, that you weren't fit to work then you would be sent back to your cell for the rest of the day.

The morning shift normally ended about 11.45 a.m. That was lunchtime and the prisoners were taken back through to the dining hall, where a head count was done again.

The lunch normally consisted of three courses: soup, main and dessert.

Lunch normally lasted for about an hour and after that the prisoners were taken out to the yard for sixty minutes of exercise. If the weather was too bad, then the inmates would be kept inside and given some free time to spend in A Hall.

It was then back to their day jobs until their shifts clocked off at 4 p.m. That was also the stipulated dinner time. Like at lunch-time, the prisoners would go through for their main meal and they would all be counted in and out.

The dinner consisted of a main meal followed by a portion of bread and butter and a cup of tea.

They would all then be returned to their cells in A Hall to allow the prison staff to get their own dinner break. The prisoners would be allowed to freshen up and to use the recreational facilities if they were entitled to them. They would be allowed to go back to the dining room, where they could watch television, play snooker, table tennis, cards, read the newspapers or just to have a chat with others. If you had lost your recreational time, then you were left in your cell.

The evenings and Saturday and Sunday afternoons were normally the visiting times for convicted prisoners. That was the only thing that broke up the monotony of prison life for some and got them through their sentences. It was a highlight for most the inmates.

Everyone would be returned back to their cell around 8.45 p.m. for their night-time cup of cocoa along with a sandwich or a bun. The cells were locked up and a final numbers count of the day would be done. The backshift staff would then sign off to be replaced by the nightshift.

That would be the process until 6 a.m. the next morning, when the same old routine would kick in all over again.

7

Rooftop Protest Leaves the Ears of Torry's Residents Ringing

There was one particular day a prisoner decided to noise up Craiginches. He had been out in the exercise yard for his daily lunchtime walk. This wayward prisoner decided to take a detour and ran out of the yard and up onto the roof of the main building just before you entered A Hall. That allowed him to get access to the roof on top of A Hall.

The situation was complicated. As a prisoner officer, you couldn't go up and simply drag an inmate back down. That isn't protocol. You have to negotiate with the prisoner and try to talk them down of their own accord. When this prisoner went up on the roof there was no talking to him, down or otherwise. He wanted to make his point and was up there all afternoon, evening and night.

We tried to persuade him to come down but he wasn't having any of it. Looking back it is quite funny, but it wasn't at the time! We had to leave a guard out all night to keep a watch on the prisoner, just in case he tried anything else or attempted to escape. Needless to say the guards were far from impressed at being exposed to the North-east elements all night.

Extra officers also had to be taken in to help in situations like this. We not only had to pay close attention to the prisoner on the roof but we also had to make sure the rest of the jail was secure and it didn't spark anything else off.

If this prisoner felt his protest wasn't having the desired effect, then he certainly found a way of becoming the centre of attention. He wasn't going to go quietly. He started to ring the prison bell in the tower at two in the morning. You can imagine how that went down amongst the local residents of Torry, especially those in the immediate vicinity of the prison, in the neighbouring streets of Walker Road, Grampian Place, Wellington Road and Polworth Road.

The longer the bell was rung you could see more and more lights going on in and around the surrounding houses; people wondering what was going on, although maybe it wouldn't have been put so politely by some of the sleep-deprived locals that early morning. If they had got a hold of the prisoner, like us, they would have probably wanted to wring the prisoner's neck – never mind the prison bell!

The prisoner quickly realised he had played a bum note or two, as the following morning he decided to give himself up. No doubt he was cold and hungry and had decided enough was enough. We got him down and he was put back into a solitary confinement cell.

The prisoner was called in to the governor's office, where he had to explain his antics. Everything was noted so staff could put future practices in place to avoid a repeat performance.

If I remember correctly, I think that particular prisoner ended up losing his remission and his chance of early release. Yet when he was eventually put back in with the other inmates he was viewed as something of a hero. When you go against the regime then you get a lot of respect for that. Some prisoners started to look up to him after that – even though all he had done was to extend his sentence.

The irony is that I don't think the whole episode was anything more than a prank. There was no chance of the prisoner making his escape from the rooftop, so you just wonder why he did it. I don't suppose we will ever know. We asked the prisoner at the time and he just laughed.

That rather noisy incident led to the bell being removed from the tower of Craiginches Prison. The governor, Mike Milne, made the order so we wouldn't have a repeat episode – much to the relief of the majority of the people in Torry on either side of the prison walls.

It was only put back up when we celebrated our centenary!

8

A Not-So-Great Escape

I recall being on duty with one of our new officers. He got a night that I am sure he won't forget in a hurry – if at all. It all started when we were walking routinely through B Hall and heard a constant tapping noise. We began to look around the cells and we eventually got to the bottom of the minor disturbance: it was one of the untried prisoners who had been trying to get our attention.

When we got to his cell he informed us that there were sheets hanging down past his cell window, all the way down to the ground. Right away I got on the radio and alerted the outside patrol of the possible breach, and the front gate, who called for police assistance and a sniffer dog.

I then went out and joined the search with the outside patrol, which normally included the officer who was in charge of the shift. We quickly scanned the outside walls and outbuildings and we were pretty confident that the escapee or escapees were still inside the prison.

A few minutes later, the police dog came in with its handler and within minutes the two prisoners were unearthed. As soon as the dog was let off its leash it got a scent of the runaways and their cover was blown. The dog just stopped, barked and looked up to the chimney stacks on the roof of the work shed. Sure enough, both prisoners had been hiding up there, hard against a chimney stack.

They knew they had been caught red-handed and they were never going to escape. There was nowhere else for them to go. So they embarrassingly jumped down from the chimney and gave themselves up.

They were put in holding cells after they had been up in front of Governor Swanson, who demanded a full explanation of the entire situation. It caused a right upheaval.

We also had to go and relocate the other prisoners from the communal cell where they had escaped from because the security there had been breached.

When we first went into the cell to investigate the possible escape all prisoners pretended they were sleeping and made out as if nothing had happened. I am pretty sure they would have known all about the escape plan but would have been well warned not to let on.

When we started to look into the escape we found they had actually wet a towel and then taken the towel rail and used them to force the two central window bars apart so they could get out. They had managed to tie sheets together to get down and they had used them to scale the wall from the third floor.

The prisoners had certainly thought long and hard about their escape from their cell but they hadn't looked too far beyond that. When we found the prisoners they had no provision to try and get over the wall and to actually get out. So I think it was more an opportunist prank than a genuine break for freedom.

9

Who Said Drugs and Money Don't Grow on Trees?

Once drugs started to come into prominence in society they also became a problem behind bars. It became a major issue in the final years at HMP Aberdeen. That was evident from the government's own inspectors. The good thing is that drugs weren't as freely available then as they are now and I wouldn't say it was a tremendously major issue at Craiginches. I think that was down to the fact that the majority of our staff was always very proactive and moved with the times. We tried to remain one step ahead of the inmates as much as we could – we always had to be very alert.

We were also in constant contact with the police to make sure that staff were kept up to date with what was going on in the drug scene. The police would often come across at lunchtime to hold regular talks with the prison staff to keep them updated on various crime issues, especially on the drugs front. The police would give us hints and tips on what to look out for and to let us know what drugs were on the go. That was important because it kept us vigilant and abreast of the changing drug trends.

The other good thing about Craiginches was that it was

such a close jail. The majority of the prisoners and officers got on well. Most of the time we knew what was on the go or what inmates were up to. Being proactive meant we were also able to act accordingly and nip things in the bud before they became a real problem. That changed a bit when some of the more hardened prisoners came down from Peterhead to finish their sentences. They were transferred because they had been threatened or their lives were in danger or they were being upgraded to another prison which was a positive step forward if they were doing a long sentence.

The main problem for us was cannabis, or 'hash', as it is also more commonly known. That was the drug that caused us the biggest headache at Craiginches. The key was cutting off the supply routes, which were via visitors taking the drugs in illegally, or outside accomplices throwing it over the prison walls. The prisoners were always searched after visits to make sure nothing had been handed over. The prison officers on duty would also keep a close eye on visitors and make sure there was no close contact or the opportunity to try and smuggle something in.

If anything was found then it was confiscated from the prisoner, and he could end up getting into further trouble, probably put on report, depending on the view of the governor.

In the worst case it saw prisoners lose remission, which would stop them getting out of their sentence early, or they could be charged with trying to get drugs into the prison.

I wasn't really prominent in the visiting area because I spent a lot of my time patrolling the halls and the gardens. We always had to do regular searches round the grounds to make sure there was nothing left lying about or thrown over the wall. It wasn't just drugs; money was another issue that used to come in illegally the same way.

The money or drugs would normally be stuck in a plastic carrier and thrown blindly over the prison wall. Often coins were tossed over the wall because they had a bit of weight to get into the prison grounds. The people throwing the packages were taking a chance because they didn't know where they were going to land. They may have had a rough layout of the grounds but they would have had no idea who was going to find it. The chances of the parcel reaching its intended party were remote to say the least, but it was a chance people were willing to take.

The other added complication was that the perimeter walls were normally planted with vegetables like potatoes, carrots and cabbage. There was also a walkway right around the inside of the prison wall. It and the grounds were always regularly inspected and so if anything was found, it would be picked up by the officers and handed to someone in control.

If it landed in the vegetable patches then it might lie a little bit longer, but if anything was missed by the officers then the likelihood was that it would be picked up by the prison handyman who looked after the grounds.

There were also times when we were tipped off about possible Unidentified Flying Objects coming over from the outside. There was a prisoner who had been sentenced to life. I got on really well with him. He kept me informed of many potential situations. There were a couple of incidents that he told me about because he had been threatened to make sure he went out and got the parcel for a certain prisoner.

The prisoner told me on the quiet and I would then alert the other officers and we would go out and search the gardens and pick up the contraband before we let the prisoners out. That way our informant didn't get the blame and wasn't implicated in tipping us off.

If you were known to be a grass or a snitch, then prison

could become a very dangerous place. Prisoners could quite often be ostracised and would come in for the cold shoulder from the other inmates. There would also be the occasional set-to and fights amongst the prisoners who tried to single out snitches.

There were also the so-called soft touches that the more influential prisoners would find and knew they could lean on and there were the inmates who used to like to stay close to the so-called top prisoners. However, the majority just got on with their everyday lives and saw out their sentences.

The problem was that Craiginches was like anywhere else. Yes, it had a bad element, but it was no worse than any other jail.

10

The Unofficial Craiginches Beer Garden

There was one afternoon when I was working in the prison gardens. We had a compost heap for all our garden rubbish but that day I noticed something wasn't quite right. It looked like somebody had tried to move quite a bit of the compost. I went and had a closer look and I discovered two large gallon disinfectant containers within it.

After I returned the containers to the control room, we quickly realised it was home brew. Some of the prisoners had tried to make their own beer and had tried to brew it in the compost heap. It just shows you have to be on your toes. Obviously, some prisoners had thought they could use the heat from the heap to ferment their beer.

I remember when I opened the containers. It smelt and looked absolutely putrid. I would hate to think what it actually tasted like! The prisoners might not have thought so at the time but I definitely did them a favour by finding their stash. If somebody had ended up drinking it they probably would have ended up poisoning themselves! It is fair to say that Tennent's and McEwan's had nothing to worry about on that particular front.

We never actually got to the bottom of who the local Craiginches brewer was. We had a fair idea but nobody actually owned up and didn't have enough evidence to point the finger. It was that bad an attempt I am not sure I would have owned up either!

SPECIAL
ASSIGNMENTS

11

FROM RIOT CONTROL TO FLYING TOILETS

I did a lot of work at the Scottish Prison Service College down in Polmont, near Falkirk, especially after I had taken a physical training course at Edinburgh University. That took me eight weeks and I was another two weeks at Loch Tay. Edinburgh University had built this special facility/hotel which specialised in outdoor activities on the banks of Loch Tay. It was owned and used by the university to teach all who attended courses, including the Scottish Prison Service. You would go there and do canoeing, hill climbing and orienteering – it is pretty much an outdoor adventure centre – but that was after you had done your eight weeks at the university first. It was a first-class facility.

There were nineteen of us on that course, including three officers from the Irish Prison Service. Another local officer who was there was a guy called George Laird, who was from Saughton Prison in Edinburgh. We went on to become very good friends during the course. He went to Glenochil Prison and then moved on to be stationed at the Scottish Prison Service College at Polmont. He was responsible for introducing all the training for the control and restraint procedure into the prison service. Control and restraint is basically a practice to make riot and prisoner control more manageable and more efficient. It was really professional and brilliant to see it in full flow. He invited me down to the Scottish Prison Service College at Polmont to train to become a control and restraint instructor. I really enjoyed learning all about it as it was a great step forward for the future for training staff on the techniques.

You would use it in scenarios where the circumstances were dangerous and you needed to regain control of the situation. Normally you would have a helmet and a shield as basic protection but there were times when you needed a little bit more.

One such scenario could be when a prisoner had maybe barracked themselves into their cell. We had a special machine that you pushed into the sides of the door, pumped it up, and then you warned the prisoner to stand back! When you pressed the button it basically took the cell door off its hinges. There was no messing about.

There was individual training and team training, as more often than not you were deployed in small teams. You also normally went into these situations in a prearranged formation. For smaller operations like for incidents in cells you would normally go in teams of three officers. The officer in the middle would have the shield and the two other officers would be on his shoulder at either side. That would allow the officer with the shield to corner the offender and then the others to come from the side and restrain him.

You have bigger teams and formations for more major issues, like some of the riots we had to attend at Her Majesty's Prison Peterhead. They were high-risk situations and at times you would have three men with shields at the front and between each shield you had three men tucked in either side. You would also have shields above the men and it was an awesome sight. More like a battle scene from an epic film like *Braveheart* or *Gladiator* than from one of Scotland's prisons.

Ironically, the control and restraint training was brought in to improve the safety of the officers and the prisoners. An inmate might not have thought it when they were faced with a control and restraint team but they were actually less likely to get hurt than if they were to attack a regular prison officer.

We also went down to England to a big open prison. I can't recall the exact location but it had an unused RAF air camp. The English Prison Service initially didn't buy into it! We started to train some of the English-based physical training instructors because the Scottish Prison Service was well ahead of them on this particular front.

I ended up at Peterhead Prison on three separate occasions, one rooftop protest and two riots. Peterhead was a far different place to HMP Aberdeen. It was mainly long-term prisoners in Peterhead. There were your hardened criminals and some of the worst offenders in the country. It was the top jail in Scotland at one point for long-term prisoners. It was also rather cruelly dubbed 'The Hate Factory'. It was the top prison until the new prison at Shotts, near Glasgow, was built.

There were times at HMP Aberdeen when we would take inmates from Peterhead, but only if we saw a definite improvement in their behaviour or attitude. They would maybe see out their time at Aberdeen or even go down to an open prison before they were eventually released.

Peterhead was a scary place. It was an experience, especially when you went in on control and restraint operations. We used to use one of the old work sheds at Peterhead to train our staff in joint exercises. You are trained for high-risk situations and scenarios. When you go in, there is a mix of excitement and a bit of fear because you just don't know what you are going to be confronted with.

When we were at Peterhead we would normally work in twelve-man teams and clear the prison section by section until the situation was brought under control and the prisoners were put back under lock and key. Most of the time it was straightforward, although not always. There was one odd occasion which I will go into later.

On one deployment to Peterhead I actually ended up dislocating my thumb. There had been a riot. The prisoners had caused havoc and had basically wrecked a wing. They smashed all the toilets and sinks and started to use them as missiles. I had been holding one of the shields at the front and the next I knew a part of a broken toilet had been thrown down from one of the galleries! It came past the side of the shield, hit my hand and dislocated my thumb. I was in agony but I know it could have been an awful lot worse. In all honesty, there was very little chance of the missile breaking the shield. I continued with the manoeuvre until we managed to get the situation cleared and after that I went and got treatment and found out the full extent of my injury. I knew I had taken a sore one but even as a trained first-aider I knew my first aid training would have counted for very little until we had got the situation under control. Such are the pitfalls of being a prison officer.

It wasn't always physical but you would have all sorts of abuse and things thrown at you. I think I have been called everything under the sun in my visits to Peterhead.

On a couple of other occasions all we did was secure the area and left it to the professional negotiators to talk the prisoners out of the situation. That was their job until we got them back in their cells.

Normally you travelled up in teams. My team was always

from Craiginches. We had a first-class training programme there because I would bring all the new stuff back from the training college and the governor would always want us to embrace it and to keep all our officers at the forefront of all the latest prison procedures.

Whenever one of the officers was off at the college I normally got the call from George through the Governor and was sent down on detachment. Officers from HMP Aberdeen were also sent to some of Scotland's other prisons, like Low Moss near Bishopbriggs. Low Moss was an open-type prison and an old RAF camp.

We used to go down there for two month detachments when they were short of staff. They used the former billets as the accommodation for the prisoners. It was mainly the short-term prisoners from Barlinnie prison who went there but sometimes they weren't any less of a challenge than the long-term prisoners. However, it was a great place to work with a good, relaxed atmosphere. There were also a lot of ex-Aberdeen staff who had been transferred to work there when it opened.

12

THE SAS DARES AND WINS

My most infamous deployment was to Her Majesty's Prison Peterhead and was back in October 1987. There had been a riot in the D-Wing of the prison. The majority of the inmates were serving life sentences.

The prisoners had taken control of the wing, which was serious enough in itself, but they had also taken one of our fellow prison officers as a hostage.

Most of the prisoners knew they were doing long sentences and had a long time to serve before getting out so they probably thought they had nothing to lose. If I remember correctly, they were protesting against the living conditions in Peterhead. Some others were also angered that they were being imprisoned in the North-east rather than in the Central Belt because it left their friends and families with a major headache when it came to visiting and travelling to see them.

The occupants of D-Wing were unscrupulous individuals who weren't to be messed with. So when they captured Jackie Stuart, the bosses knew he was in significant danger. It is a situation that is every prison officer's worst nightmare. You know there is a risk when you sign up, no matter how small.

You just hope and pray it won't ever happen and if it does then not to you!

I had been deployed up to the 'Blue Toon' several times on special assignments. On this occasion, we knew something serious had happened when the prison authorities informed us to get a team of control and restraint officers organised and our riot equipment into the van and get to Peterhead as quickly as possible, as there was an ongoing incident – that was all we were told. We were quickly organised and ready, so we set off not knowing what to expect, but aware that all our training may soon be put to the ultimate test. When we arrived we were given a briefing about the situation and were located up on the first landing within a cell so we were ready if we were needed. It was just a case of waiting. We were made aware that they had taken a hostage and were on the roof of the prison but we did not learn who it was until later on that day. We knew how serious a situation this was and we just had to be patient. The prisoners were holding all the aces. Our team just had to remain on standby and await further instructions.

It was left to trained negotiators to try and get the prisoners to release Jackie. Their efforts continued to fall on deaf ears and it was clear we weren't getting anywhere fast. Our time was spent drinking tea and coffee and keeping everybody's minds occupied to save the team getting bored as we never knew when we would be needed. At the end of the day we were relieved by another group of trained staff so it was off home with an early start the next morning, but the longer it went on it become clear that maybe more drastic action would be needed.

We had just taken up duty early the next morning and we were sitting in the cell when it all kicked off. There were several explosions and flashes and there was smoke everywhere and within a few minutes the prisoners were being marched down the stairs one by one to the ground floor by SAS soldiers. We had been sitting on the front line but unknown to us a rescue plan had been hatched – we did think amongst ourselves earlier that the longer it went on some drastic action might be needed. The good news was that Jackie was safe. The prisoners were returned to prison custody and then transferred to several different prisons around Scotland.

The SAS had obviously looked at plans of the prison well in advance and worked out the best way to get Jackie out. The operation had been done in style, precisely and without any fuss. I was there and I had a job working out how it all happened, as did the members of my team.

We later learned that the SAS soldiers had been flown up from RAF Lyneham to do the job. We stayed on at Peterhead for the rest of the day to assist them with getting the prison working again as normally as possible. That is a chapter that neither Jackie nor myself or the members of our team will ever forget and I was more than happy to be returning to normal duty at HMP Aberdeen.

ABERDEEN FC

13

We're Not on the March with Ally's Army!

Ally MacLeod will certainly go down as one of the most colourful characters that Scottish football has ever seen. The bubbly Glaswegian managed Ayr United, Aberdeen, Motherwell, Airdrieonians and Queen of the South but is most famously remembered for his infamous short spell in charge of Scotland. He helped guide the national team to the 1978 World Cup Finals and his infectious nature had the country eating out of the palm of his hand.

It was only Scotland's fourth appearance at a World Cup Finals and they had previously never scraped past the first round. That is a disappointing statistic that still remains in place today. Yet MacLeod had not only guided Scotland to Argentina but also managed to stir up a tidal wave of optimism in the process. He whipped up such a frenzy that Scotland weren't heading to South America to make up the numbers, they were going there to win the World Cup!

Scotland, thanks to the somewhat dodgy vocals of the Scottish comedian Andy Cameron, another regular visitor to Craiginches, really was on the march with Ally's Army.

The cult single peaked in the United Kingdom's Top 10. The fans were looking for even more success on the field. The expectance hit home when more than 25,000 disciples of the Tartan Army pitched up at Hampden Park to cheer Ally and his players off on an open-top bus en route to Prestwick Airport. It was a tradition normally reserved for teams who had already won silverware – not in advance of it happening!

The feel-good factor, however, burst quicker than a balloon. MacLeod and his team were embarrassed by Peru and were then held by Iran before they signed off with a much-needed win over Holland. However, that was too little too late and Scotland were eliminated on goal difference. The team and MacLeod returned home humbled and instead of the World Cup all they could offer was a bucket load of broken dreams! If a lot of Scotland fans could have had their way, then Ally could well have been facing time in Her Majesty's Service for his so-called crime against the nation. MacLeod did keep his job but only for one game before he had to bow to public pressure and end his reign in shame.

The whole sorry episode did bruise MacLeod's ego but in his usual upbeat way he wasn't to be downbeat for too long. He was soon back in management, grabbing even more national column inches and headlines with his outspoken comments, along with some of his teams' performances on the pitch. People say MacLeod's unique mannerisms would have enabled him to sell ice to the Eskimos or sand to the Arabs! Yet there was one hard-to-please audience that, by his own admission, he failed to win over – the A Hall of HMP Aberdeen!

The charismatic football boss made his visit to Craiginches during his time in charge at Pittodrie. During his two year spell at Aberdeen, from 1975–77, MacLeod lifted the League Cup. Many believe he laid the early foundations for Sir Alex

Ferguson's glory run with the Dons before he took the Scotland job. Billy McNeill succeeded him for a year before Ferguson went on to weave his magic that made Aberdeen not only the pride of Scotland but also kings of Europe – when they toppled the mighty Real Madrid in the 1983 European Cup Winners' Cup final.

MacLeod certainly made a real impression in his short stay in the North-east, although there were many of our inmates who thought his patter was criminal. You might be wondering how we actually managed to get one of Scotland's top managers behind bars – albeit temporarily.

It all came about because there were three or four local pensioners who would tidy up Pittodrie after all the team's home games. They would pick up all the rubbish, sweep up and just clean up the mess left behind from all the supporters. It used to take them the best part of a week and it was a bit of a thankless task but the pensioners enjoyed it because they were big Aberdeen fans and they wanted to do their bit for their club. It was also a way of keeping them active and on the go, and giving them a wee bit of income into the bargain, as they were all official employees of Aberdeen Football Club.

It was through the then chairman, Dick Donald, and the club's legendary kit-man, Teddy Scott, that we got some of the prisoners involved. I was a long-term friend of Teddy's. I had got to know him from doing my referee training down at Pittodrie. We used to do all our workouts on the Pittodrie car park and over the years I started to become friendly with Teddy. He knew I worked at Craiginches and he broached the subject about some of the prisoners coming down to help at the stadium.

I thought it was a cracking idea that would be good for the football club and also for the prisoners. It would give them an incentive to get out and about, and as far as I was concerned it was a win-win situation for everyone. So before we took things any further Teddy went to the chairman and Mr Donald gave us his full blessing – he was behind the idea. So I then went to our governor at Craiginches, Scott Ogilvie, and we quickly got an agreement in place.

Pittodrie was one of the first outside ventures of this type we had at the prison. The governors then just let us get on with things, although there were pretty stringent guidelines, as you would expect, for taking prisoners outside of Craiginches. I would never take more than four prisoners out to a project at a time. And if I couldn't get four prisoners that I felt I could trust then I would take fewer people. I also knew that I had to limit the prisoners to four because any more and we would have needed another prison officer and that just wasn't feasible.

So I would go down with three or four prisoners and help them to clean up the ground. We would all meet after breakfast and a van would take us to Pittodrie at about 8.30 a.m. It would come back for us at about 3 p.m.

We would do the same work as the pensioners but because there was more than double the number of hands, we could not only get the chores done quicker, but we were also able to do a lot more in the same timescale. The work that normally took a week was suddenly done and dusted in two or three days. Once we had finished inside the ground we would head outside to the car park behind the Main Stand to clean up the rubbish there and even do the weeding to keep things ticking over.

Mr Donald was a true gentleman and he thought it was something special getting prisoners to come down and help his club. He would always come out into the Main Stand to say hello and ask how we were getting on.

The prisoners also loved it, working in a football ground.

It brought them into contact with some of their heroes. There were the likes of Bobby Clark, Arthur Graham, Drew Jarvie and Davie Robb there at the time.

I didn't really know Ally MacLeod that well but I asked Teddy if there would be any chance of the manager coming in to do a question and answer session at Craiginches. He said: 'You clean the ground for him, so I don't see why not! Leave it with me.' Teddy, true to his word, got hold of him and we asked the question. Ally was great. I said we would give him a wee tour of the prison and then it would really make the prisoners' day if he would sit down and have a wee chat with them at the end of it.

Ally didn't have to be asked twice and right away he agreed. We then got a date that suited everyone. He came round the prison with me and I got the feeling he was quite taken aback. He even said: 'It is nice in here'. But I joked: 'I'm not sure the permanent prisoners would share your view!' He just laughed.

I then asked him if he would maybe talk to the prisoners for half an hour in the chapel but in typical Ally style he said: 'Half an hour! I will manage a lot longer than that!' He was true to his word and answered every question. You have to remember that it wasn't just Aberdeen fans he was facing. There were Rangers and Celtic fans, and supporters from just about every club you could imagine. So you could say it was a very unforgiving environment. Even the Aberdeen fans, when they weren't looking for the inside track, were telling him he was picking the wrong team! It was a really good evening and after about an hour I actually had to tell Ally that it was time up. He probably would have been more than happy to sit there all night talking to the prisoners but we had to get them back in for their tea before we got the cells locked up for the evening.

I said: 'That is time up, Ally." He replied: 'Oh, how time flies.' One sharp-witted prisoner immediately piped up and shouted: 'Speak for your bloody self!' It left the rest of the prisoners in stitches and even Ally had to laugh. It didn't stop him from signing a few autographs before he headed off into the North-east night.

Ally later mentioned his visit to Craiginches in a newspaper article. MacLeod may have seen it as a way to try and add to Aberdeen's popularity over the longer term but it is fair to say his charm offensive never quite came to fruition on the inside.

MacLeod, speaking in the national press not long after, said: 'I have appeared on television seven times since my move to Pittodrie. I've spoken at nine meetings, including a talk to the convicted inmates last week at Craiginches, and I've spouted thousands of words. The idea is to win back the support and it's working. The red and white scarves are appearing again on the streets of Aberdeen.

'Of course, it may be some time before any of the inmates of Craiginches are available as supporters, but they'll get out eventually and you could say my talk there was long-term policy. I enjoyed the experience but I was glad to get out!'

14

HELPING THE DANDY DONS TO NET GLORY

There is no doubt the link between Aberdeen Football Club and the city's prison was considerably strengthened by our work in helping the pensioners with their regular Pittodrie clear-ups. That agreement remained in place for a good couple of years before it eventually became too much for the pensioners in their more advancing years.

It was a big job and so the chairman, Dick Donald, decided to bring in other people to do the work. We were more than happy to continue but I think he and the club felt uncomfortable with the fact that the prisoners were doing the work for nothing. He was an honourable man and obviously felt it wasn't right. He didn't want to look as if the club was taking advantage of the prisoners or the situation.

I didn't have a problem with the club's decision because we had so many other things coming up and it let us and the prisoners concentrate on them.

Though there was still a need for some of the captive skills from Her Majesty's Prison Aberdeen because some of our prisoners also made and mended just about every sort of netting. The Pittodrie groundsman had shown me the nets one day on one of my regular visits to see Teddy. They were torn and ripped and were in serious need of repair. They had clearly taken too much abuse from the goalscoring talents of Joe Harper and his fellow Aberdeen stars – not that you would have had too many complaints from the Pittodrie faithful for seeing too many home goals.

I immediately said that we could repair them for you in the prison. The groundsman just looked at me in bemusement. I then explained we had prisoners who actually made football nets in our work sheds. We were already supplying them to a number of senior clubs, such as Montrose and Brechin City, and a load of other Highland League and local junior clubs in the North-east as well.

It wasn't just football nets that we produced in the prison. The prisoners also made fishing nets for the boats and trawlers. We also used to repair them as well, which could be a big job at times, depending on the battering they had taken at sea.

We were lucky that lots of our local prisoners had worked on the boats and were able to repair the nets and pass on their skills to fellow prisoners.

They might have been inmates but they were all highly skilled at their jobs. They not only made the nets for the fishermen but they also supplied netting for the military.

We did different things in the work sheds. We had a lot of major craftsmen, especially in the joiner's shop. We had a top joiner. Anything you could make with wood he would produce – from benches to seats and tables to even more obscure things that had to be custom-made. Nothing was a problem.

The prisoners might have come in with some skills or limited knowledge or ability but regardless they were taught different skills in the workshops and made the most of them. The majority of the prisoners took a great pride in their work. They also knew if they did put in a shift then the day would pass a lot quicker. If they decided to muck about and not pull their weight, then they knew it would be a long day.

We had a sectioned off part of the work shed where the knitting machines were, for making all the staff uniform jumpers. Ten to twelve prisoners were employed there at a time. We also had a shoe repair shop where a party worked repairing shoes, etc. It would employ around six to eight prisoners.

We had a joiner's shop where all types of wood products were made – may I add to a very high standard. Here they would again employ six to eight prisoners. We also had a works department that usually employed three prisoners to work with the tradesmen doing maintenance in the prison. The kitchen would employ around ten prisoners to help prepare the food, serve it up and then attend to all the washing up afterwards, along with and keeping the dining room clean and tidy. In A Hall they would have about six pass men for keeping everything clean in the hall showers and toilets. We had a trusted prisoner who worked in the staff area and muster room, keeping everything clean and tidy, and upstairs in the office they would also have a pass man who kept everything clean. He also kept the office staff and the governer supplied with their tea and coffee. There were trusted prisoners working in the gardens seeing to all the vegetables and mowing the grass in the prison and the prison quarters outside. The reception also had a trusted prisoner for keeping the place in order and doing the laundry. Out in the grounds a trusted prisoner would empty all the rubbish bins from the various departments and burn everything in the incinerator.

Mr Donald at Aberdeen FC got wind of our work – particularly our net making. The Aberdeen chairman told me not to bother getting their old nets repaired because he wanted us to make a new set. The prison went on to make and supply the football nets at Aberdeen from Ally MacLeod's era up until Sir Alex Ferguson was the manager.

Mr Donald and his family owned the Capitol Theatre in Aberdeen. It was the main venue where all the top acts performed and he gave me permission to approach any of the acts attending to see if they wanted to come and visit the prison or perform there. However, when acts were only there for a one night stand it was no good. I also became quite friendly with Billy McNeill. Billy had taken over as Aberdeen manager from Ally MacLeod. He had come in from Clyde after a more than glittering playing career with Celtic and Scotland.

Billy might have lifted the European Cup with Celtic and is one of the most decorated stars in Scottish football history but you would never know that by speaking to him. There are no airs and graces with him and he is such a gem of a man. He is a lovely, lovely guy and would do anything he could for you.

Billy had a house down in Stonehaven when he moved to the North-east and he wanted me to come up with ideas for his garden to improve how it looked. He didn't like the layout and so I set about trying to put something together. I was more than happy to help the likes of big Billy out.

I suggested he move things around and give it a bit more colour and Billy was delighted with my suggestions, but it was quite a big job and I was quite relieved when he said he would get contractors out to get the job done, which he did.

That bit of work did earn me a bit of currency with Billy, which I was able to quickly call in – although I am sure the Aberdeen boss would have done it regardless. I asked Billy if he would be willing to come up and do a night with the prisoners. I told him Ally MacLeod had come up before him and the night had been a roaring success. I forgot to tell him about the stick that Ally took from the prisoners! I thought that was better left out because I didn't want to scare him off!

True to his word, Billy came up to Craiginches for the night. He also brought along a few well-known faces with him for reinforcements in the shape of top Aberdeen stars Bobby Clark and Drew Jarvie. The fact that Billy was manager of the Dons and had played for Celtic meant he was going to get it from the Rangers fans rather than from all sides like Ally!

It helped that Billy was doing such a great job at Aberdeen. Things were really taking off at the Dons but any success he had at Pittodrie was never going to go unnoticed, especially from his former employers, Celtic. The call every Aberdeen fan dreaded did eventually come, just over a year into his Aberdeen stay. Sean Fallon had struggled to step out of the shadows of Jock Stein, after he had left for Scotland, and so they turned to their former captain, McNeill, in 1978.

I was actually with Teddy Scott at lunch when it all kicked off and it was certainly unknown to me, if not Teddy! The two of us were sitting on a bench outside the old gymnasium with a cup of tea when big Billy and John Clark came through and announced they were leaving Aberdeen. They had just been in a meeting with Dick Donald and the board and had told them they wanted to go to Celtic.

Billy had done a great job but the call of his first love, Celtic, was just too much for him to turn down. The Pittodrie hierarchy couldn't convince him to stay and he headed to Celtic Park for the first of his two spells there. It was a shame to see him go because I firmly believe that if Billy had stuck around he would have brought real success to Aberdeen – much the same as his successor, Alex Ferguson, who we will talk about a bit later.

Billy may have moved on but Teddy ensured that I remained the green-fingered friend to everyone at Pittodrie throughout the years.

I also got friendly with the Aberdeen striker Davie Dodds in the late 1980s. It was the same old story! He had told Teddy he was looking for somebody to help get his back garden in order. It was an awful mess when he moved into his house in the city's Broomhill Road. Teddy immediately volunteered my services. I am still not certain to this day whether he was on commission or not! He asked me the question and so I went up and had a look. We had to dig everything out and then he wanted a vegetable patch with some flowers at the side. I knew it was not going to be a big job but Davie had vowed to help me. Davie is a lovely lad but I quickly realised I would be quicker and better doing it myself.

So that is how I got to know Davie and his wife, Jill, and we have continued to remain friends long since he hung up his boots. They were both up for our Silver Wedding when Davie was still a Rangers player.

Davie was another person I got up to the prison. He insisted it wasn't a problem and said he would also rope in his fellow striker and the former Scotland, Celtic and Arsenal star Charlie Nicholas. They came up and did a question and answer session.

Davie and Charlie were brilliant. They were like a comedy act, with the pair constantly contradicting themselves and taking the mickey out of each other and their teammates. Charlie took pelters because he turned up with this long black leather jacket on. He said it was the same coat as Bono, the lead singer of the rock band U2, was wearing at the time but Davie and the prisoners weren't having any of it.

Charlie insisted he had bought it from a boutique in London when he had been down at Arsenal but he got stick because it was so long. Davie and the prisoners kept telling him he must have had to kill about seven cows to get enough leather for the jacket! In fairness to Charlie, he took it on the chin and also gave as good as he got! The prisoners lapped it up, spending time with some of the players they worshipped or supported every week.

Aberdeen stars Craig Robertson, Jim Bett and Robert Connor were amongst some of the later visitors to Craiginches. They did an hour-long question and answer session with the inmates.

Bett admitted: 'It's certainly nice to visit the men inside and try and let them forget their troubles for a short while. It's also nice to know you are coming out the same night.' Flame-haired midfielder Robertson hadn't long joined the Dons from Dunfermline back in 1988 when he came up.

He joked: 'I didn't expect to be in prison so soon after coming to Aberdeen. I must say it was nice to be asked and this is the only way to do prison!' I know we were lucky to get so many big names from Aberdeen to visit the prison through the years. They all gave their time for nothing but I know the time they spent with the prisoners was invaluable.

When we got something organised then we would put up posters in A Hall to tell the prisoners what was happening and when. Every time we did it, especially when it was anybody connected with Aberdeen Football Club, it brought a real excitement to the prison. It was the same when we announced a musical or social event. The inmates looked forward to them because it got them away from the normal routine and broke up what could be a pretty mundane existence behind bars. It gave them something to look forward to. I think it also helped that Aberdeen FC were a major force in Scottish football at that time as well!

15

Fergie Tells Us We Will
Beat Real Madrid

There is no question that 11th May 1983 will go down as the greatest day in Aberdeen Football Club's history. It is also one of the most memorable nights in Scottish football history: when the dandy Dons brought the might of Real Madrid to its knees. Yes, Real Madrid, one of Europe's greatest-ever sides, had lost to a team from the North-east of Scotland – who had never won a European trophy before.

The scenes from Ullevi Stadium in Gothenburg are still etched in the vivid memory of every Aberdeen supporter of a certain vintage, whether they were in Sweden or glued to their television screens. The image of Mark McGhee swinging in a cross for super sub John Hewitt to go diving in the rain to head past Spanish keeper Agustin and give the Dons their famous extra-time 2 – 1 win will never be forgotten.

The win had looked on the cards after Eric Black had scored in the seventh minute, although those early hopes were quickly extinguished by a short pass back that led to a penalty and saw Juanito equalise from the spot for the Spanish superstars.

Yet you could never write off an Aberdeen team managed by Sir Alex Ferguson. He had almost single-handedly, along with some help from Jim McLean at Dundee United, helped to smash the vice-like grip that the Old Firm, Rangers and Celtic, had long since held over Scottish football.

This was an Aberdeen team who had gradually evolved and boasted top quality players like Willie Miller, Jim Leighton, Alex McLeish, Gordon Strachan, Neil Simpson, Neil Cooper, McGhee and Black, to name just a few. The majority of the boys had come through the ranks or had been cherry-picked from smaller clubs. These players, under Sir Alex's guidance, had taken the Dons to a new level. They were not only one of the top teams domestically but they had also proved to be a top European outfit that flew the flag for Scotland with real pride.

To get to the 1983 European Cup Winners' Cup they saw off Swiss side Sion, Dinamo Tirana, Lech Poznan and Waterschei but there was no doubt that the big win came in the quarter-finals when Sir Alex's team saw off the mighty Bayern Munich. That result came as a result of a 3 – 2 victory at Pittodrie after a goalless first leg in Germany. That landmark win gave the Dons, the Red Army and Sir Alex the belief they could beat any team – even the mighty Real Madrid!

The result and win over Real not only put Aberdeen on the European map but it also sent shockwaves round the world, although not necessarily in the Glennie household. Yes, there were wild celebrations and delight, as there were in many homes throughout the north-east of Scotland that night, when Willie Miller triumphantly lifted the European Cup Winners' Cup to the rain-filled Gothenburg skies, but everyone in the Glennie household was always confident that Sir Alex and his team would be bringing the famous old trophy to the Granite City.

In fact, Sir Alex Ferguson himself had told us in our own living room that we could beat Real Madrid. We had become very friendly with Sir Alex and his wife, Cathy. They would come round to our house at the weekend. Sir Alex came in one Saturday night and asked if it was okay if he could take a phone call. I said: 'No problem, you know where the phone is, just go and use it whenever you like.' I never asked any more, it was none of my business and I knew Sir Alex was a busy man trying to deliver even more success at Aberdeen.

Cathy and Sir Alex loved to pop round but it was important that everything was low-key. They didn't want or like to be the centre of attention. They just wanted to spend time amongst friends. That was the way the Fergusons were and still are. Sir Alex might be one of the most iconic names and faces in British sport but he has never let any of his success or achievements go to his head and that says a lot about him. He is a true gentleman with a steely determination to succeed.

Sure enough the phone went later that evening and Sir Alex went out and answered. He was probably away for about twenty minutes and then came back into the living room. He opened the door, walked back in and immediately said: 'We can beat them, Archie says we can beat them!' He had been waiting for the phone call from his long-term assistant, Archie Knox. We weren't sure what Sir Alex was talking about but then he revealed that Knox had travelled to Spain on a spying mission to watch Real Madrid play domestically ahead of the European Cup Winners' Cup final.

Archie certainly called it right. His confidence wasn't to be misplaced. Real Madrid might have been managed by the legendary Alfredo Di Stéfano and boasted world stars like Uli Stielike, Johnny Metgod and José Camacho but Sir Alex and Knox knew they had a squad of players who feared no one, and reputations meant nothing!

By the time we had got back to our cups of tea Sir Alex had us believing that Aberdeen would beat Real Madrid. So you can only imagine the belief he installed in his players – the ones who would have to go out and at least match Real Madrid!

It was a night and a game that every Aberdeen fan will never forget. It will live forever in the history of Scottish football and I am lucky enough to say I have my own personal memento of the night. The chairman, Dick Donald, gave me my own official limited edition Adidas team jacket. It was one of the same jackets that Sir Alex, his staff and team had worn on the bench that night in Gothenburg. Mr Donald presented me with the jacket a week after they came back. I have to say it is something I have treasured ever since.

It was a great touch from Mr Donald, and Sir Alex was very similar. He is also a real people's person. He was brought up the hard way and even now he is at the top he never forgets his roots, the people who helped him and friends he made along the way. I can vouch for that because every year, without fail, Sir Alex and Cathy still send a Christmas card. That continued even after he called time on his managerial career with Manchester United. That, for me, shows the mark of the man that Sir Alex is.

It is actually quite a bizarre story as to how I became friends with Scotland's greatest ever football manager. It wasn't long after Sir Alex arrived at Pittodrie from St Mirren in 1978, taking over from Billy McNeil, long before he had been knighted, when we first met.

My old friend Teddy Scott came up to me when I was in at Pittodrie and said: 'Alex is looking for somebody to do his garden and keep it tidy, can you help him out?' It was as simple as that. He got us together in the boot room at Pittodrie. Teddy introduced us and we just got on really well from that moment on. From there, I agreed to look after his garden out at his home in Cults.

Alex had that much on his plate managing Aberdeen that he didn't really have time to do his garden. Anyone who knows Alex or has worked with him will tell you that he works 24/7. He knew to be successful you had to put the hard graft in and Alex certainly did that at Aberdeen and then at Manchester United. His professionalism and standards were two of the many reasons why he was so successful.

I would go out to Cults every couple of weeks and cut the grass and maybe plant a few shrubs or flowers here and there. I grew most of them myself so it wasn't a problem. It was an easy enough job to maintain it because he didn't have the biggest garden at the back, most of the work was done out the front.

Alex offered to pay for my services but I refused from the off. A penny never changed hands but Alex always made sure I had two centre stand tickets for every game, home or away. It didn't matter if it was Cappielow, Ibrox or Celtic Park, there were always two tickets available for me. He would give me a shout at the start of the week and just say: 'We are playing such and such this week ... if youse are going I will leave a couple of tickets for you.' It was great because one of my daughters, Jacqueline, who is still a real diehard Aberdeen fan, never missed a game. But we were not always able to take up his offer for away games because of the shifts I worked. I knew if she found out we had been offered tickets then we were going and that was the end of it! We were lucky because even when it came to big European games or cup finals we always paid for our tickets but you always knew Alex would have made sure you had first class seats in the stand.

I was out doing his garden one Sunday afternoon when Sir Alex came out and said he was going away down to Perth. It wasn't until the next day I found out that Sir Alex had signed the striker Frank McDougall from St Mirren.

McDougall was the man Alex thought would be the ideal replacement for Mark McGhee, who had decided it was time for a new challenge and had headed to Germany to sign for Hamburg. McDougall proved to be another decent bit of business from the Aberdeen manager, who had unearthed more than his fair share of gems in his success-filled time at Pittodrie.

McDougall hit the ground running. He prolifically hit twenty-four goals in twenty-nine starts for Aberdeen as they went on to retain their League Championship title. McDougall followed that up with twenty goals in thirty-four games the following season but his hopes of netting any Pittodrie goal records were cruelly killed by injury. He struggled with a back injury that saw him eventually have to hang up his boots after making just one appearance in the 1986 – 87 season. Injury may have forced McDougall to retire but he still holds Aberdeen's record for goals to games ratio and shows what an eye for a player Sir Alex had and probably still has.

It was through doing Sir Alex's garden that I got to know Cathy and the rest of his family, the boys Jason, Mark and Darren. Cathy also became friendly with my wife, Hazel, and the kids, Lesley and Jacqueline, and it wouldn't be unusual for them to be round at our house, like that evening Sir Alex took the phone call about Real Madrid from Archie. Cathy was a very informal person and didn't like to make a big thing and I think that is why they enjoyed coming round to visit friends. Our kids loved it when the Fergusons came around.

We even became friendly with Cathy and Sir Alex's extended families when we used to go down to Hampden for cup finals, which were a pretty regular occurrence when he was at Aberdeen. We stopped in at Bishopbriggs to pick up Bridget and John, Cathy's sister and brother-in-law. They were a lovely couple and so sincere. They were great company and we became very good friends with them.

From Bishopbriggs, they would then guide us into Toryglen to Cathy and Bridget's mum's house. When we got there Cathy was normally already at the house. The hospitality we got there was just amazing, they were so welcoming; it was second to none. Before the match there was a full spread of soup and sandwiches and after the game we would go back and there was even more food. The spreads that Cathy's mum, Mrs Holding, put on would have feared you. They probably could have fed the whole town! We would then drop Bridget and John back at Bishopbriggs and then head back to Aberdeen – although it has to be said the journey always seemed shorter if we had won!

My problem was that even if I hadn't wanted to go to a cup final I didn't have any option thanks to Jacqueline. The one cup final that always sticks out for me was the 1982 Scottish Cup. They beat Rangers after extra-time. John MacDonald had put Rangers ahead before Alex McLeish equalised. It was a tight affair and in my heart of hearts I didn't think we were going to do it. But then Mark McGhee and Gordon Strachan scored in extra time before Neale Cooper sealed it with the fourth. I think I just remember it because I feared it was one that was maybe not going to go our way.

It was also the first major cup Sir Alex won at Aberdeen, although he had already lifted the Scottish title in the 1979 – 80 season. I remember after that cup final we were invited round to Cathy and Sir Alex's house for a celebratory get-together. We all got our pictures taken with Cathy and the Scottish Cup. It was great for the girls. We really did feel like part of their family.

Sir Alex was also very supportive and once or twice he

and Cathy came to our prison dinner dances and he would often hand in a signed shirt or something for many of the fundraisers we would have in the prison through the years.

But as they say, nothing lasts forever and Sir Alex was always destined to move on. He certainly had more than enough opportunities before he did decide it was time for a change. I knew in advance that Sir Alex was leaving and his next destination would be Manchester United. I was out doing their garden at Cults when Cathy informed me that Alex had agreed to go to Old Trafford. I was delighted for Sir Alex because it was a great opportunity for him, although I was disappointed to see him leave Aberdeen because he had done a great job for the Dons and more than anything he was a good friend. But when you know Sir Alex you quickly see how ambitious a man he is. He always wanted to be the best and he felt this was his opportunity. It is fair to say, the way things panned out at Old Trafford, he was right!

He always said to me that there were only two clubs in Britain that he would leave Aberdeen for. One was Manchester United and I am certain the other one was Tottenham Hotspur. He had built something special at Aberdeen and I think it would have been near impossible for him to leave Pittodrie for any other Scottish club.

When Manchester United came calling it was a slightly different proposition. They were one of the biggest names in world football but, by their standards, had been in the doldrums. They were something of a sleeping giant and it is fair to say Sir Alex more than awakened United, putting them back at the forefront of the English and European games.

I remember going in to see Teddy Scott not long after Cathy had told me about Sir Alex's pending departure. News had started to filter out and in all honesty Pittodrie was like a morgue. It was as if somebody had died. Teddy was disappointed as well but had a similar outlook to myself. He was disappointed to see Sir Alex go but knew he had done a great job at Aberdeen. He had produced minor miracles and had taken Aberdeen from nowhere to one of Europe's top teams. How could anyone begrudge him the chance to try and revive one of the biggest names in English football?

I continued to do Alex's garden even after he had gone to Manchester United. I would go over and cut the grass and keep it tidy for Cathy and the kids until they all eventually moved down south with Alex. I was sad to see them go but it is fair to say Manchester United quickly became the second result the Glennie household starting looking out for, after Aberdeen of course.

I always knew Sir Alex would be a success at Old Trafford. The only thing that surprised me was that it took him so long to find his feet. However, after that initial FA Cup win in 1989 – 90 he never really looked back. He went on to win thirteen English Premier League titles, five FA Cups, four League Cups, another European Cup Winners' Cup and two Champions League wins.

He has also managed some of football's greatest players such as Cristiano Ronaldo, David Beckham, Eric Cantona, Ryan Giggs and Paul Scholes. The success they had under Sir Alex again shows how good he is at getting the best out of people and delivering success as one team!

He had one of the most pressurised jobs in football but he would always have time for friends and good causes. I remember I was playing for the Scottish Prison Service against our English counterparts at bowls in Gartcosh, just outside Glasgow. Sir Alex said he would be in Glasgow that weekend and he would come and present the trophy and meet the teams but then something cropped up. He called me on the Wednesday and said he wasn't able to come but he had sent up a signed Manchester United shirt in the first-class mail. We ended up auctioning the shirt after the game and we got big money for it to help boost the funds for our SPS Bowling Association. It was a great gesture from Sir Alex because he could have quite easily said that he couldn't make it and just left it like that but he didn't. He sent us the shirt and that just shows the class of the man.

We have remained in touch. Cathy and her sister Bridget came up for Jacqueline and Gavin's wedding and we were also invited to Mark Ferguson's wedding – Sir Alex Ferguson's oldest son. We still keep in touch with Christmas cards. I know if I ever need him then I just have to get in touch and it works the same for me. When I started to work on my book, I wrote to Sir Alex to see if he would be prepared to do my foreword. In typical Sir Alex style, he called me back and couldn't have been more helpful – although he explained to me I had to wait until his own book was out of the way! I know I am lucky to know one of the greatest managers British football has ever seen but I am even luckier to be able call Sir Alex, Cathy and their family true friends. That for me is the most important thing!

THE SOCIAL WING

16

PRISON FIGHTS

You get plenty of fights and scraps in British prisons every day. Skirmishes are always breaking out amongst fellow prisoners. There is always a bit of natural aggression amongst a lot of the prisoners, especially those sentenced for some of your more violent crimes.

The majority of the time the set-tos are done and dusted within a matter of seconds and the prison officers quickly step forward to restore the peace. If you see people every day and you don't necessarily get on with them there is always going to be friction, and being in prison that can build-up over a period of days, weeks, months or even years. It is even more so in an all-male prison were testosterone levels are bound to be at an all-time high, more so amongst the prisoners who are vying for the title of the so-called top dog or kingpin.

I have also seen a fair bit of hand-to-hand combat of my own, being a former boxing referee. I officiated all over Scotland, at venues like the Music Hall and Beach Ballroom in Aberdeen, the Caird Hall in Dundee and Glasgow's Kelvin Hall. I was lucky enough to get the chance to officiate at many Scottish title fights, including greats like Tony Kerr and Alex

McIntosh of St Mary's and John Gillan and Norman Houston of Aberdeen ABC.

I got the best view in the house from inside the ring – most of the time!

I would have to say the highlight of my refereeing career was when I took charge of some of Harry Johnstone's bouts. Harry was the North-east Championship and Scottish flyweight champion. The big thing for me was that he boxed out of my home club, Insch Amateur Boxing Club.

I also officiated at many of the boxing shows in the city and surrounds and all across Scotland. I really enjoyed refereeing and I know what a disciplined and skilled sport boxing is. A fighter might be born with natural ability but they have to work hard on their fitness and their fighting techniques.

I had officiated at dozens of fights and they were always big favourites, especially with the Aberdeen public.

It had always been at the back of my mind as to whether or not we would be able to stage a boxing show at Craiginches for the prisoners. I knew it would be something different for the inmates. It could help break up the boredom of prison life and give them something to look forward to.

So I decided I would make my move, with the thought nothing ventured nothing gained. I was sitting having a cup of tea after a show one night with Robbie Kidd from Hayton Boxing Club and Adam Smith from Aberdeen Boxing Club.

We were talking about some of the bouts from that evening's card and then as the conversation progressed, I thought I am going to chance my arm here! We all gave up our time to boxing completely free. The officials were completely dedicated to the sport and gave their time up for nothing and the referees did the same. They all just loved the sport and working with the lads and passing on their experiences from their boxing backgrounds. I approached Robbie and Adam and said: 'As a wee bit of a thank you, do you not fancy coming up to the prison and putting on a boxing show one Sunday afternoon?' I wasn't sure how Robbie and Adam would react. They looked at each other and then there was a slight pause before, thankfully, and much to my relief, they both agreed it was a good idea, albeit in somewhat more unusual surroundings than they were used to.

Robbie immediately said: 'I will tell you what I will do. I will give you my ring and as long as you arrange to collect it and set it up then you can have it free of charge. You just pick it up and get it set up before the Sunday show, get everything else organised and we will get the fighters across.' So we thrashed out a date between us and got all the finer details ironed out for the big Craigie boxing show.

Prisons had held boxing bouts before but the last one in Scotland had been fifteen years earlier. So it was good we were getting the chance to put the fight scene back on the prison map.

The day before the fights I went and got the ring picked up. We set it up in the prison dining room and organised makeshift dressing rooms for the fighters from Hayton Amateur Boxing Club and Aberdeen Boxing Clubs. The prisoners, more than a hundred of them, all came through from A Hall for the show, buzzing with excitement. I was also the man in the middle. I refereed the show myself to ensure there were no major costs for the afternoon.

It turned out to be a win-win situation for everyone involved. The prisoners got the chance to see some excellent fights and were royally entertained. It also gave the boxing clubs the opportunity to give some of their younger, up-and-coming fighters the chance to go out and battle and to get some much-needed experience in the ring, away from the public eye.

The fights were a tremendous success. There was a real buzz in the air after the event. The prisoners were all talking about the fights for days after. There was no doubt it went down a storm. Even the fighters loved it although I think our kitchen staff also had a helping hand in that. They would feed all the fighters after the shows. They would serve up pies, peas and chips for them. I am not sure it would be the recommended diet for top fighters today but it certainly fuelled those boys back then!

It went down that well that we organised several other fights including an inter-club match between Hayton and Aberdeen ABC, and other bouts where a few youngsters travelled from other parts of the North-east to take part. All in all, if you pardon the pun, our boxing shows proved to be a bit of a knockout!

17

That's Entertainment

We had hosted sporting nights and events and thought it would be good to try and branch into music. Music like sport was a release from prison life, with inmates listening to the latest singles on the radio.

We knew if we could get a group to play then it could bring another form of prison entertainment. The problem, we were well aware of, was actually getting a band or group to agree to play at Craiginches. What would they be facing and how would they be received?

A local group, the Stan Fraser Band, was famous in and around Aberdeen at that time. They were a four-piece rock group who did a lot of cover versions and had an excellent following, selling out venues in and around the Granite City.

I was at a function they were playing at and I got speaking to their frontman Stan Fraser. So I explained to him that I worked at the prison and we were looking to put a few more events on for our prisoners. I asked if he and his band would be interested in playing and in a bizarre twist of fate we got lucky. It turned out that Stan, ironically, used to be the paperboy for Craiginches in his schoolboy years. He delivered the prison newspapers not for the individual prisoners but for general use. So when he got over the initial shock of the question he was more than happy to take up my offer. When I first asked him he sort of looked at me, as if to say, you really want us to play in the prison? When he realised I was being serious he thought about it for a few seconds and then said: 'No problem, we will do it.'I asked him what the costs would be, but he was adamant they didn't want anything. The entire band did it for absolutely nothing and that was our first entertainment night in the prison that didn't have a sporting theme. The prisoners couldn't believe it. Their previous entertainment had been in-prison games or activities and so this was a break from the norm. It was a real highlight and one they really appreciated. The night was a roaring success and the band got a standing ovation.

A delighted Stan Fraser, speaking to the *Evening Express* about his visit in 1987, said: 'We did not know what to expect but, obviously, the lads seemed to appreciate us and we would definitely do it again if the prison wanted us back. It is quite different to the venues we normally play but we enjoyed it and would like to thank the prison authorities for inviting us.'

The feeling was pretty mutual. The Governor stated: 'This is our second year of live entertainment. It breaks up the monotony of jail life for the inmates. They love it. We want to make the jail part of the community. We want to do things for the town and, hopefully, it will do things for us in return so that the individuals in Aberdeen feel they are not forgotten.'From there I thought we should try and do events like that more often and so things snowballed.

We had a karaoke night that was hosted by the then Northsound disc jockey John McRuvie. John's voice is commonplace on the Aberdeen airwaves and now he is on Original 106. I remember talking to him as I escorted him back out and he told me that was something he would never forget. We also got a few local bands in, like the Sandy West Quartet, and the comedian Bob Weir. Then we were able to take things to a whole new level.

18

Songbirds and Jailbirds

Musicians and the wrong side of the law can often go hand in hand. Some of the greatest and biggest names in music have spent time behind bars.

The likes of Chuck Berry, Sir Paul McCartney and Rolling Stones pair Mick Jagger and Keith Richards have all done time. Jagger and Richards spent just one night in custody on drugs charges before they were released on bail the following day but spending time inside certainly seemed to be rock 'n' roll for many.

Artists who have done time can be like a *Who's Who* of music. Outrageous Sex Pistols bassist Sid Vicious was arrested after his girlfriend, Nancy Spungen, was found dead in his New York apartment.

Wildman Ozzy Osbourne might be more famous for his television appearances now but in his wayward past had several stints inside. Serving time has helped so-called stars live up to their bad-boy reputations, although it is fair to say Sir Paul McCartney doesn't exactly fall into that category, although he was arrested in Japan for a drug offence.

Boy George and the late George Michael are two other

high-profile offenders who have spent time behind bars, courtesy of Her Majesty's Prison Service.

At HMP Aberdeen we also had our fair share of 'performing celebs' – although I have to make it clear from the start that none of them broke the law! They all came to the prison of their own accord.

We managed to persuade a few well-known faces to come in and perform at Craiginches. It all snowballed from the early boxing shows, football visits and other events we organised and put on at the prison through our Community Links Committee.

We thought it would be a good idea, if possible, if we could take things to another level. We knew Aberdeen was a popular tour destination, thanks to the Capitol, The Music Hall and other top venues it could boast, like the Lemon Tree. We thought it might be worth trying to see if some more well-known stars would consider playing on a slightly more off-beat stage.

It certainly didn't do much to derail the career of the late Johnny Cash. The legendary American country and rock star starting performed in American prisons in the 1950s. He kicked off at the San Quentin State Prison and continued to play various detention centres across the States. It also led to him recording two of his most famous albums *Johnny Cash at Folsom Prison* in 1968 and then a similar record back at San Quentin a year later.

Other more current British stars like Wet Wet Wet frontman Marti Pellow has performed at HM Holloway Women's Prison while Billy Bragg is another, having played at HMP Dorchester.

Arguably, one of the biggest names we had at HMP Aberdeen actually came to us: Toyah Willcox. Toyah first broke on to the music scene as part of the New Wave of music which hit our radios and television channels in the 1970s to mid-1980s. She fronted her own band simply named Toyah before she embarked on her own successful solo career with her biggest hits being 'It's a Mystery', 'Thunder in the Mountains' and 'I Want to Be Free'. Toyah then branched into television and was a household name having appeared in popular shows like *Minder* and *Tales of the Unexpected*. She was also cracking the big screen in the cult film *Quadrophenia*.

So we couldn't believe our luck when Toyah pitched up at the gates of the prison one day. She was touring in the city and decided to pay Craiginches a visit. The staff certainly didn't have to be asked twice to give her a tour and it is fair to say she left more than a fair few happy faces, from the staff to the prisoners.

Toyah then told us that when she toured she liked to go and visit local prisons and young offender's units. She admitted it was unusual but she got a wee kick out of it. She just milled about and spoke to the prisoners. They couldn't believe their luck!

When we told her that we actually held regular live gigs and social events for the prisoners she told us she hadn't realised or she would have played a set for them. She then promised the next time she came up to Aberdeen she would do a live show in the prison.

We weren't sure if she was just paying us lip service but she was true to her word and we didn't have to wait too long before she was back in the Granite City, starring in Peter Shaffer's *Amadeus* play at His Majesty's Theatre.

So Toyah got in touch and agreed to come up to the prison to do a live show for us. She did a tribute gig to the late American singer-songwriter Janis Joplin, who tragically died of a drug overdose.

It was ironic but I thought there was a decent message from the show and Joplin's downfall which Toyah depicted in her show.

I was quoted in the local press as saying: 'There might be a message for the prisoners.' Toyah's visit caused a bit of a media flurry with headlines like 'Toyah plays to a captive audience', 'Tragic tale behind bars' and 'Key roles for Toyah' in the local Aberdeen press.

The day came and Toyah came up to the prison that afternoon with her band.

Toyah had to get changed and it is fair to say we didn't have many female options for her in a primarily all-male prison. I ended up taking her to the chapel so she could get changed. I put her in behind one of the confession boxes and as I waited it gave me a chance to tell her about our entertainment programme of concerts, Burns suppers and the Pensioners' Christmas party. I also told her about the work we did on outside projects with the prisoners. She could hardly believe it and she said: 'That's fantastic.' Then Toyah appeared dressed and ready to perform to her waiting and adoring public.

She must have done a live set for about an hour, doing all Joplin's most famous numbers, like 'Piece of My Heart' and 'To Love Somebody'. The prisoners loved it and lapped it up. She signed off by signing a few autographs and gave a few lasting memories to some inmates who thought they might never have seen the likes again.

It is fair to say Toyah got a kick out of it as well. She did an interview with a newspaper after her visit and said: 'The audience in Aberdeen was very focused on what was going on and when you see they are enjoying the show, it gives you the energy to carry on. Doing this show around prisons is the most precious and rewarding thing I have done in my career because it is done to purely communicate with people and not simply for a wage packet. In saying that, it is not the easiest or most enjoyable thing I have done because it is not like theatre work. You are playing to a single sex audience with a lot of tension in the air.'

Our very own Evelyn Glennie was another visitor to Craiginches. We were fortunate enough to get the North-east percussionist to the prison a couple of times. The first time was in 1990 and she came back a second time three years later. Her return was part of a special tour that British Telecom sponsored. They wanted to bring artists to more offbeat venues that maybe couldn't attract or afford the bigger name artists and took them the length and breadth of Scotland from Stornaway all the way down to Dumfries. If I remember correctly, Evelyn did ten dates as part of our tour and every date was completely sold out – well, the ones you could buy tickets for anyway!

The other off limits date she did, outwith Aberdeen, was at a young offenders institute in Dumfries.

Evelyn was big, big news at the time. She was not only a talented musician but she had also been awarded her Officer of the Most Excellent Order of the British Empire (OBE) in the New Year before her visit to Craiginches in 1993. That title was then upgraded in 2007 to Dame Commander of the Most Excellent Order of the British Empire (DBE).

Evelyn, even today, still remains one of the world's top percussionists – despite the fact that she has been totally deaf since she was a child.

Her second visit was more hands-on. She signed autographs and posed for photographs and then she played a short set and held a special workshop with the prisoners and taught them how to play some basic notes on various percussion instruments. The fact that the prisoners were more hands-on made it even better for them.

Evelyn, speaking at her visit, insisted: 'Music is a marvellous medicine for all human beings. I don't see why we should exclude people who are in prison. I think we need to try and help prisoners rather than just shut them away. Music can affect them in a deep way.' Country star Dominic Kirwan certainly can't be classed as a songbird but in the country and western circuit he is certainly up there with the biggest names in his genre. The Irishman was another we persuaded to come to the prison. I managed to get a hold of Dominic through Jim Rosie and Moira Fraser. Jim used to stay beside us and he had a music shop in the city. They knew a lot of artists. He told me Dominic was coming to Aberdeen and he would ask him if he would play at the prison. Sure enough Jim came back to me and said Dominic was more than happy to come up to the prison.

I have to admit I was more than a little concerned the day he was due to come. He was twenty minutes late and there is always a bit of doubt at the back of your mind as to whether or not they will really turn up.

I was thankful because if he hadn't arrived we might well have had a riot on our hands and I would have been the one getting lynched. We had also invited the Maidencraig young disabled group from Woodend Hospital up for the show. So I would have felt awful if Dominic hadn't appeared.

Dominic, much to my relief, did arrive with his five-piece band. He was really apologetic and then told us he had been late because he had been struggling to find somewhere to get his laundry done.

So I sent Dominic to go and get set up and I told him I had the perfect solution. I went down to see our prison reception laundry chief, Tam. I asked him if he could sort out Dominic's washing. He said no problem and took it. The only problem was that because Tam was still in the laundry he missed most of Dominic's concert and he wasn't happy! He came in with his washing as Dominic was playing his last number. Tam turned and said: 'Bugger that. I have just done his washing and I've not heard one song!' So I went up and explained the situation to Dominic and asked him if he could play another couple of tracks. I told him his washing would be dried and ready to go by then! So he played another couple of songs and everybody left happy.

Dominic's appearance led to coverage in both the *Press and Journal* and *Evening Express* newspapers. Dominic was quoted as saying: 'I am not used to singing in the afternoons but it was good craic and I hope the guys enjoyed it as much as I did.' Some of these artists were at the heights of their fame when they came to the prison. It really was a great touch coming up to entertain the prisoners on a completely voluntary basis. They never cost us a penny other than the washing powder for Dominic Kirwan's clothes! All joking aside, I also don't think the likes of Toyah, Evelyn and Dominic realised just what an impression their visits made.

To many of the prisoners it would have been the highlight of their time inside and would have brightened up some otherwise sad existences.

That was summed up by a former HMP Aberdeen governor, Bill Rattray, who was once famously quoted as saying: 'Events like these help to improve the quality of life for the men. That is why we always try our best to get bands and artists to perform at the prison.' The only artist we got knocked back from, ironically, was Toyah Willcox – although it wasn't directly from her! She came back up to the North-east and was playing a gig at Stonehaven. I went down to the venue to see if I could catch a quick word with Toyah. When I asked if there was any chance of speaking to Toyah, the lady at the desk just looked me up and down and then said: 'Just buy a ticket like everybody else!' I didn't pursue things any further as I only wanted to meet her again and tell her about my book.

19

Robbie Shepherd, Haggis and Prisoners with Knives

I thought it would be a good idea to hold a Burns supper. Burns night is always a big occasion in Scotland, as people get together to celebrate the life of one of its favourite sons, the poet Robert Burns, or the Bard as he is also affectionately known.

I thought it would be good to organise our own supper because we could also get some of the local community involved. I spoke to the governor, Bill Rattray, and the kitchen staff, mainly Norrie Page and Gordon Tough, as they had most of the work to do, but I knew I could depend on them. They were all really enthusiastic and up for it. Whatever they served up at whatever event always seemed to be a big hit with all our visitors.

So we got organised and decided that it would be a good idea to invite some of the local pensioners along. I had a great rapport with Ted Munro, who ran the local old age pensioners association, St Fittick's, in Torry. So I approached him. He was delighted. He asked the men and women involved and they were all really keen to come along to the Burns supper. The only problem was that we had to limit the numbers for security reasons. We needed a number that could be easily controlled, especially if anything happened. We settled on about thirty visitors and then allowed Ted to put out his chosen invitations. Things went well and it didn't take him long to fill up all his slots. By all accounts, he had to leave a few people disappointed but we were hopeful this would be the first of many and others would get the opportunity to come along to future Burns suppers.

There was a fair bit of planning to get everything organised for the supper, from the setting up of the dining room to the kitchen staff preparing the food and getting the entertainment booked and arranged.

We even managed to pull off a major coup to get a big name to address our haggis at that first Burns supper. I managed to get an article printed in the *Press and Journal* newspaper where I cheekily asked Robbie Shepherd if he would toast our haggis. I didn't know Robbie at all, so it was nothing more than a shot in the dark.

Robbie, as everyone knows, is a Scottish icon. He was born in Dunecht but is a real champion of the North-east of Scotland. He was famed for his broadcasting on Radio Scotland and his traditional Scottish dance music show, until he announced his retirement in 2016. He has also written his fair share of books in the mother tongue of the North-east – Doric.

It was a bit of a punt on our behalf but it was a case of: 'If you don't ask, you don't get.' What was the worst case scenario? Robbie could only say no or not get back to us at all. What was there to lose?

Luckily enough we found Robbie to be the perfect gentleman. Sure enough he saw the article and got in touch with me. He asked me the details of the Burns supper, checked his diary and his commitments and then came back and said he would be delighted to attend.

It was great news for the prison, the pensioners and everyone who was involved in the organising, knowing that this was going to be a Burns supper with a real difference!

Robbie did the Burns supper that first year and toasted our haggis in some style. He absolutely loved it and came back every year to address all our future Burns suppers. He was great company and the pensioners and prisoners all loved him because he was such good fun.

It was important that the prisoners also felt a part of it because it was all about them. We got one of the inmates, Tam, to play the part of the famous Robert Burns character Holy Willie. We dressed him up all in white and we gave him a candle and his own Bible to make him look the part. He loved it despite being labelled 'Holy Willie' by some of his fellow prisoners. He was even given his moment of fame as he was quoted in the *Press and Journal* newspaper saying: 'I read a wee bit of poetry and I'm doing all this for a wee laugh. I'm a bit of an extrovert, so I don't think I'll be nervous when I get up to read the poem.' He did well reading out Holy Willie's prayer and the Selkirk Grace. A lot of real hard work was done behind the scenes by everyone.

The only thing the pensioners had to do was to turn up on time. It would be like any other night out for them, but we asked them to leave any valuables or handbags at home. We know that some might have needed their purses or wallets for bus fares, but if that was the case we made sure they were locked up safely at the front entrance. The last thing we wanted to see was anything going missing or being stolen. It would have caused us a lot grief with the prison service and if there were any problems then it would have made it harder for us to organise similar events in the future.

Thankfully, that first night went like clockwork. Everything went to plan. We welcomed the pensioners, sat them down at their tables and then brought in the prisoners to join them before the haggis was piped in.

'Holy Willie' then read out his poem, Robbie addressed the haggis and then we did the traditional toast – although whisky was substituted for orange juice in the only real change from your traditional Burns supper.

We then let a prisoner loose with a big knife but there was nothing to fear because it was just for use on the haggis. We then served the haggis up with neeps and tatties (swedes and potatoes). After the meals had been finished off we cleared the tables and then allowed the pensioners, staff and prisoners to finish things off with a dance. That was normally in front of some very good entertainment acts. That first night we had Pam Dignan's Dancers and the Ian Menzies Dance Band. In later years we had the Horizon Dance Band and also welcomed Iain MacPhail, who had his own Scottish dance band. He was another big name in the Scottish dance band scene, up there with Jimmy Shand. He was involved in the union of the prison officers. Iain initially made contact by writing to me. He had heard about our Burns suppers and asked if he would be able to attend the following year. I told him we would love to have him as long as he brought along his accordion and promised to play for us. He came back to us and thought I was joking, as he didn't even realise we had live music at the supper.

There was another year during the early '80s when Rangers weren't exactly setting the heather alight in Scottish football. The Aberdeen supporters revelled in it, as their team were not only conquering Scotland but Europe as well. I remember one of my friends, an officer from one of the Central Belt prisons who I knew very well, sent me up a poem to be read out at one of our Burns suppers.

It read:

O' Lord heap blessing on the soup,
Heap blessing on the stovies,
Heap blessings on the Papes and Jews,
The Muslims and Jehovies.
Heap blessings on all gathered here,
On absent friends and strangers and if you've any blessings
*   left*
For Christ's sake help the Rangers!

As you can imagine it went down a storm. The Aberdeen fans were delighted to make fun of one of their great rivals.

The Burns suppers at Craiginches continued for a number of years and were a great success. It was good to celebrate the life of the bard – rather than prisoners being barred from all contact outside the prison walls!

We also invited the pensioners along for a few Christmas parties. That was an extension from the Burns supper. Local performer Hyldie Grinstead came along with some of her fellow musicians from the local scene and provided the music for our Christmas parties. There were thirty pensioners from the local Torry pensioners group who were invited in for their Christmas dinner and a party. Hyldie was also given some unusual backing in one performance. Hyldie recalled: 'The atmosphere at those parties was great. The prison governor, Mr Rattray, even got up and sang and played his guitar.' We sat the pensioners down and gave them their three course dinner. Then one of the prisoners would come in all dressed up, sometimes in a Santa Claus outfit, and walk in with the big Christmas cake that had been made for the day. The cake was cut and was then served up after the meal with their tea and coffee.

Then the boys would come through from A Hall and the pensioners and prisoners would be up dancing. It was great to see. Everybody saw that the afternoon event was a real highlight and you could see everyone really enjoyed it, from the staff to the prisoners and our esteemed visitors, and the success of the event was down to the prison catering staff, who never ever let us down at events like this.

20

Get that Rangers Fan Behind Bars!

Andy Cameron (MBE) behind bars. Now that is a sight many people would pay to see, especially Celtic and Aberdeen fans who have been at the centre of his merciless jibes since he started his legendary stand-up routine.

The Glasgow-based comedian has long been one of Scotland's favourite and most-loved comedians. His razor-sharp wit and killer punchlines means that when he is in full flow nothing and no one is safe or off-limits.

The funnyman was probably made famous for the Scotland World Cup 1978 single 'Ally's Tartan Army'. It came out at the time when the team qualified for the finals in Argentina on the crest of a wave under Ally MacLeod – another Craiginches visitor – brainwashing the nation that his team were going to come back as world champions. I knew that Andy had done a few prison visits before and I thought it would be worth trying to get him up to Craiginches. Andy had entertained the masses at Barlinnie, Cornton Vale and Peterhead and I was hoping he would add Aberdeen to that list.

The football visits and music nights had been very popular and I was in no doubt Andy would be a smash hit with the inmates.

So I wrote to Andy personally and asked if he would be willing to come up to the Granite City. I wasn't sure because he is a massive Rangers fan and I knew that coming up to Aberdeen was like entering the lion's den for him. Aberdeen had been the main challengers to Rangers in the late 1980s and early 1990s and there was and still remains a massive rivalry between the two teams and sets of fans.

I wasn't sure what response I would get but I was pleasantly surprised. Andy wrote back and said he would be delighted to come up and do a gig at HMP Aberdeen. He was first class and said he would do it free of charge because he always liked to give something back to the prisoners.

Andy, speaking to *Aberdeen Journals*, explained his reason for giving up time to the Scottish Prison Service. He said: 'Why do I do it? Well, let's face it, it could be me or any of us sitting in there. We're just kidding ourselves if we think we couldn't end up in a place like this. You can get into trouble very easily when you're young. Some teenagers rebel against their parents, others get political but many go into crime. Obviously, you have got to take some of the blame yourself for ending up in a place like this, but very often the blame can go other ways as well. I'm here now and I can walk out but these guys are here to stay and that's punishment enough. Whatever these guys have done, you have to remember they all have people who love them.' Andy came up to the prison and was given a guided tour by the governor, Leslie McBain, and myself, and then he took to the stage where he entertained more than ninety prisoners for more than half an hour.

Nothing was off limits and everyone got it whether they were from the world of politics, religion or football. Andy set the tone early on when he opened with a joke that went something like this. 'Knock, knock' with the usual response 'Who's there?' Andy replied: 'Terry Butcher' – the legendary Rangers

111

and England captain who was one of the players Aberdeen fans loved to hate. That was met with a chorus of boos and a few defiant cheers from the Rangers amongst our inmates.

The prisoners also didn't get off lightly. Andy joked: 'Nice woman the Queen. Have you ever met her?' The obvious reply was: 'No.' 'Oh, you never go out then?' He also likened Craiginches to a decent hotel.

He said, with more than a wry smile: 'They've got it good. Three square meals a day and a roof under their feet.' Andy also tailored his sets for specific audiences. He did his homework on Aberdeen and then let fly. Speaking about the Mastrick area of the city, he sniped: 'It makes Easterhouse look like Beverly Hills.'

The stand-up had also been up to Peterhead and knew its rival town was Fraserburgh. 'The Broch' also came in for some close-to-the-bone stick. Cameron cheekily said: 'They don't have a village idiot up there. They just take a shot each.' One of the biggest cheers came when Cameron slaughtered the waiting press photographers who were taking pictures of him and the prisoners for the following day's newspaper.

He laughed: 'You can break the ten Commandments quicker than you need to take a photograph.' There was no doubt Cameron's visit injected some much-needed humour into Craiginches. He certainly helped to lighten the mood on his visit.

Governor Leslie McBain admitted: 'Having a personality like Andy Cameron coming here means a great deal to the men.'The final words, however, end with Andy himself, when he stated: 'What I get out of it is seeing the guys' eyes light up with a little bit of hope when you make them laugh.'

21

THE WHISTLEBLOWERS

When you speak to football fans from most clubs or leagues in the world, they will tell you that the performances of referees and their assistants at times can be criminal. I can personally vouch for that. Not as a frustrated Aberdeen fan but as a former referee. You are the man in the middle and at times you can also be the centre of attention. You might want to go through the game unnoticed but there are times when that is never going to happen, especially with at least twenty-two highly charged players going head-to-head before you even throw in managers or the coaches. You are never going to leave everyone happy at the end of a game.

It can be a thankless job at times but I got a lot of enjoyment from my refereeing career. I officiated a lot of games in the juvenile, amateur and school leagues in and around Aberdeen. I was a linesman, or an assistant referee as it is called today, in the Highland League.

I remember one game in particular at Kynoch Park many years ago. I can't remember who Keith were playing but the visitors were needing every point they could get to keep them top of the league. The referee was from Aberdeen and the other linesman was a minister from the Huntly area, I can't remember his name. The game ended in a draw and they were needing the win to remain top. Afterwards there was a lot of criticism being made towards the match officials but we just headed to our dressing room and closed the door. However, the shouting still went on and we could hear it even with the door closed. Then they started kicking the door until someone actually put his foot through one of the panels of the door. He had some job getting his foot back out but when he did he soon took off and we heard no more. The damage to the dressing room door was reported to the Keith officials and we went on our way home.

I made a lot of friends through refereeing, from managers to players, but especially amongst my fellow men in black.

We all used to train together every week in the car park at Pittodrie. That, as I said earlier, was the reason I got to know Teddy Scott and managed to strike up such strong links with Aberdeen Football Club through the years.

One of the main people on the Aberdeen refereeing circuit was Sandy Roy. I got to know Sandy really well. He was a top referee who officiated at the very highest level in Scottish football. He made a real name for himself and is still highly respected in the game. Sandy has done a power of work for refereeing in Scotland and especially in the North-east. Even since he hung up his whistle he has continued to dedicate himself to refereeing. He was the Scottish Football Association's manager for Aberdeen referees and today he can still be seen in the stands at Premiership games as a refereeing supervisor, marking today's officials and giving feedback to their Hampden boss.

I knew how popular football was within the walls of HMP Aberdeen. There was always football in the prison on a Wednesday night and on Saturday afternoon in the exercise yard. It was very competitive. It could be anything from six-a-side to eight-a-side. Everybody took the game seriously. Sometimes the games would be physical and not for the faint-hearted because everybody wanted to win, and it also gave the prisoners the bragging rights and the upper hand in the banter stakes in the run-up to the next game.

We had a sports day every year and at the end of it we always had a football match. It normally ended up Aberdeen versus Glasgow. So it would be the prisoners from the North and North-east against a team of prisoners who were from the Central Belt but were serving time at Craiginches. That always added a bit of spice to those matches.

Radios were also on, especially on a Saturday afternoon, as the football-loving prisoners waited to hear how their team were getting on. It was quite funny, especially when there were times when maybe their hall had been locked up for the night. All you could hear was the commentary from the radio and suddenly there would be a massive roar and that was normally when Aberdeen had scored. You also had it when Rangers or Celtic scored against the Dons and the banter started to fly! We knew how much the football meant to the prisoners and the threat to stop their matches or to ban their radios was enough to keep most of them in line.

The visits from the managers and players at Aberdeen were extremely popular so I thought if we could get some of the referees involved it would put a new twist on things.

The prisoners might have been shown the red card from the judicial system but I thought this would give them a different viewpoint on the game. I decided to sound some of them out to see if it would be worth putting a night like that in place and of course the resounding response was yes. I then went to Sandy and he agreed to come up and put a visit together for us. I thought he was a brave man coming to talk to a roomful of prisoners but then again after refereeing in front of 50,000 at Parkhead or 45,000 at Ibrox I suppose everything else, including a visit to Craiginches, would be a walk in the park.

Sandy put on a really good show. He had to put up with a lot of good-humoured banter and by the time he had finished he had been everything from a Celtic and Rangers fan to just about every other club in the senior Scottish leagues.

Despite all that, Sandy was pleased with how things went and it led to another visit. This time, we managed to get another of Aberdeen's top referees, Billy Reid. I also had the added luxury that I knew Billy because I had actually worked with him in the machine shop at Barry Henry Cook.

Billy came along to the prison with the legendary Aberdeen goalkeeper Bobby Clark. He gave a talk about his refereeing career and there was a fair bit of banter, with Billy giving a referee's perspective and Bobby giving his view as a player. It was quite funny and a decent insight into the game from both sides. As most football fans will know, it is very rare that the teams, managers and their fans will see things the same way as the officials. More often than not, refereeing decisions cause a lot of headlines and controversy in the game. As a former referee, I have every sympathy with our officials. I also know that officials can become an easy target for players and managers to deflect their own deficiencies. They also know that referees and their assistants can't say anything back.

Billy and Bobby both went down well on their visit. Everybody agreed that it had been a good night and we thought it would be good to arrange a few more similar events, going forward. The foundations were in place and the goodwill was there on both sides, but when I got back to work I realised that the prisoners might want to take things a step further.

A couple of them came up to me and said they would be really interested in taking a referee's course. I knew it would be no use to them when they were serving time but I agreed it would still be a good thing to do. A good skill to have and something they could use after their release. So I spoke to a few others and word started to spread like wildfire. It was clear there was a real interest so I went to Sandy Roy to see if there was anything we could put together.

Sandy was brand new but, to his credit, thought it was a great idea. I went back and spoke to the inmates and we managed to get a course put together. I think the Scottish Football Association also saw this as a good tool because it had been the first of their courses that had been run from behind bars. The problem was that we needed to limit the number of prisoners on the course so we agreed to cap it at six. That was more manageable and meant we didn't need to draft additional staff in for the classes. So we kept the prisoners who had put their names forward informed of what was happening, they did the course and they all enjoyed it.

Sandy came along once a week and put them through their paces. It was exactly the same course that the SFA put in place for everyone who wanted to go into refereeing. It was basically the laws of the game and how you should referee a game. They were put into various workshops and scenarios before they all had to do their referee's exam at the end of it. The prisoners passed them with flying colours. They even made the local press and our newest recruits showed off their newly inherited red cards through the gates at Sandy.

I know Sandy really enjoyed putting the course on and was

pleased with the overwhelming response he got from the prisoners. I am not sure if any of the prisoners did put their newly learned skills into operation but at least when they left Her Majesty's and went back into society, they had another string to add to their bows.

Who Said Crime Doesn't Pay?

22

Outpost for the Outlaws

Burn O'Vat is a popular nature reserve in the north-east of Scotland. Officially it is called the Muir of Dinnet National Nature Reserve, although it is better known locally as Burn O'Vat. It is something of a natural phenomenon, as it dates back more than 15,000 years ago to the Ice Age.

Lochs Davan and Kinord meet there and it is also home to hundreds of rare species of birds, insects and animals but the true centrepiece of the site is the 'Vat'. It basically looks like a giant pothole but has far more significance, as it was formed due to the glacial meltwaters. The disappearing glaciers left a catalogue of remains, meltwater channels and kettle hole depressions that have turned Burn O'Vat into such a natural treasure chest.

The Vat also has history of its own. It is claimed that the sixteenth-century Scottish outlaw Patrick McGregor, or Gilderoy, as he was also often referred to in Scottish literature, used to hide out at the Vat. McGregor was a less glamour-ised version of his namesake, although no relation, Rob Roy McGregor.

He led a band of limmers (or robbers) who ravaged the lands of Aberdeenshire, Cromarty, Braemar and Strathspey.

It is claimed McGregor went on the run after he killed his own mother and turned to a life of brutal crime, robbing and stealing whatever he could. A price was quickly put on his head and he soon became a man in demand, forcing him and his brutal gang to operate from the criminal shadows, as they stole everything from livestock to more valuable commodities like money and jewels.

The Vat was a hiding hole for McGregor as he tried to escape from angry pursuers or the authorities. There is a shallow impression behind the main waterfall of the Vat which he used as his cover and is now known as Gilderoy's Cave.

So you might ask, what has all this got to do with Her Majesty's Prison Aberdeen? Well, Burn O'Vat actually helped to put Craiginches and some of our prisoners into the headlines for all the right reasons! Like McGregor all those hundreds of years before, they had broken the law and fallen foul of the authorities – but our prisoners used Burn O'Vat to give something back to the local and surrounding community.

It all came about thanks to a chance meeting. My wife, Hazel, loves it up at Burn O'Vat. We quite often go up there for a day out or a run in the car. It was on one of those visits that I bumped into a man called Ian Watt, who worked at the nature reserve. He now stays on the other side of the world, in Moonta in south-west Australia, and we still keep in touch to this day.

We were just having a general chat. He asked me what I did and I told him I was a prison officer, and I then went on to explain how we were trying to open things up to get a bit more interaction between the prisoners and the public. The entertainment nights within the prison had been a start and something we had been looking to build on.

Ian then asked if we fancied coming up and doing some work with the prisoners at Burn O'Vat. The nature reserve welcomes thousands of visitors through its doors every year. People enjoy days and nights out, searching for anything from rare water beetles to otters, while the rich woodlands are home to many breeding birds like the chaffinch, wood warbler or the slightly less well-known Kentish glory moth. Each Scottish season also brings something different, as the winter attracts many migrating birds, gees and wildfowl.

That is not to mention the many man-made additions that Burn O'Vat can proudly boast, including a hut on stilts – a crannog, as it is also known – that was built during the Iron Age and still sits on Lock Kinord. There is also a ninth-century standing stone, along with the remains of hut circles and medieval moated homesteads.

It is such a vast site, more than one hectare in size. Yet despite having such a rich history, all the way from the Ice Age to modern times, with many things built or added or left as they were, the one thing that was sadly lacking was a simple walkway.

There had been traditional dirt paths but they were hardly ideal for visitors, especially those with young children or those who needed access. The reserve wanted to install walkways or ramps but due to a lack of funds was struggling to finance the project and the work.

So Ian asked, if they provided the materials and transport, would we be willing to put a team of prisoners together to work at Burn O'Vat over a period of time, just before and then after the main visitor season.

When we left Burn O'Vat that day, I felt a real buzz of excitement but it was still nothing more than a good idea. A lot of water had to flow under the bridge before it came anywhere near fruition.

I thought it was a great opportunity for the prisoners but I knew the final decision wasn't down to me! I went back and spoke to the prison governor, Scott Ogilvie, as I knew that taking any inmates outside of the prison had to be cleared by him. He would also need to get authorisation from his own bosses, like we had to do for our Pittodrie work, and after that we would then need to see if any of the prisoners would want to get involved.

Luckily the governor shared my enthusiasm for the project. He saw the merits of it and also knew, if it was successful, that it could help show HMP Aberdeen in a slightly better light!

So after speaking to his bosses no objections were raised and we were given the green light. We both went up to Burn O'Vat to look around and to see what work the people at the reserve wanted to be done, for example those walkways up to the viewpoint. Most of it was old-fashioned manual labour! Some half-decent joinery skills would also come in handy, although that wasn't a necessity of the job description. As we came to the end of our trip the governor turned and asked me my thoughts and I said: 'Why don't we just give it a go?' Thankfully, he agreed and Operation Burn O'Vat was born.

The governor told me I could take out a team of prisoners. We agreed on a team of four because I knew that was a number that was controllable. I would normally speak to some of my fellow officers before we decided the team who would do the work. We needed people who we knew would put in a shift but would also be trustworthy and wouldn't cause us any trouble. This project was a major breakthrough for the prison and the inmates and we all knew that if anything went wrong then there would be no second chances.

It was a big job but the nature reserve gave us all the raw materials we needed. We would leave about 7.30 a.m., just after breakfast, and be up at Burn O'Vat around 8.30 to 8.45 a.m., depending on traffic. We would work until 3 p.m. so we could get the guys back to the prison, to allow them to get showered and ready for their dinner, as their only other meal of the day would have been a packed lunch.

Burn O'Vat also provided the transport for us and the prisoners to get up and down every day – a Range Rover.

It was certainly anything but a day out for the prisoners. Yes, it was a privilege and they may have been outdoors but they had to work hard and probably put in more of a shift than if they had remained back at the prison for the day. Yet that was a small price to pay just to get some freedom and to be outside rather than being cooped up in a cell or spending their day in the work shed.

We ended up returning to Burn O'Vat bi-annually over the space of six years to get everything for the project all done and finished. Our first visit was normally in early spring before the main visitor season kicked in. We would work for a couple of weeks and then we would go back and do a few weeks in September after things started to die down a bit. We would do a bit of tidying up, maintenance and burning before we continued with our work on the walkways to the viewpoint and back down to the car park.

Anyone who has been to Burn O'Vat will be aware that the vat sits on ground level and then about 200 yards across the burn you can then start climbing the hill up to the viewpoint. The nature reserve wanted a wooden walkway laid down either side to reach the viewpoint, as you looked down the loch at Dinnet. The first year we built the walkway up one side and the following year we laid the walkway coming back down from the viewpoint.

I have to say, seeing the project take shape over the years gave me a tremendous feeling. I knew the work the prisoners had put in – and all those involved certainly put in a real shift. It is fair to say they did themselves and the prison proud with their work at Burn O'Vat.

That was pretty much summed up by this little story. We were doing the walkway coming back down the hill towards the car park at the time. It was a fair distance, a good few hundred yards. I remember one of the nature reserve staff, Jim Parkin, said, 'I know there is a fair bit to go but don't worry about it. Just do what you can, we aren't expecting you to finish it all!'

That was a fair assessment because I thought I would have had to keep the prisoners out night and day to get it done in that time frame!

It wasn't just a case of just throwing down the timber and hammering the walkway together. There was a massive amount of preparation work that went in before we even got to that stage. We needed to level the land underneath because it was really uneven. Some parts you walked at your own risk and I am not sure Health and Safety had got to Burn O'Vat at the time because there really were some treacherous underfoot conditions, hence the new walkways!

Normally two prisoners would work at the front doing the preparation work and then the other two would work at the back hammering the decking or wooden frames with me. Some of them may have had carpentry skills from their previous lives but for some others this would have been their first experience, but it didn't take any of them long to get into full swing.

The prisoners had obviously been listening to our conversation about the walkway and the fact we weren't expected to finish it all the way down to the car park, and I think that was the extra motivation that they needed: 'Don't underestimate us.' My foreman in the group had been at Burn O'Vat with me before and he knew exactly what work had to be done. He said: 'Right, lads, let's get this job done.' By the end of the Tuesday the other lads had a grasp of the job in hand and it was all go. At the end of the first week I did think we might make it but made no comment. The second week was a hard slog but, my God, they just kept on going and come Thursday I knew we were nearly there. On the Friday Jim paid us a visit again and was astonished to see the job completed to our usual high standard. He congratulated the lads individually for the wonderful job they had done. Jim's speech was all the motivation that the lads needed and I myself was very proud of the job they had done: mission accomplished.

I remember another time at Burn O'Vat we had finished the walkway we were doing on the Thursday before lunch-time. We all went back to the reserve HQ depot to report to Ian Watt, one of the wardens, that we had finished. He was busy trying to renovate an old outbuilding which they wanted to make wind and watertight to house all their tools, equipment and machinery. We worked with Ian for the rest of the day and all day on the Friday. When we finished we had got all the repairs done and there was just the roof to do, so I went back to my bosses at the prison and asked if they could spare us another couple of days to get the job finished. They agreed, so we went back on Monday and Tuesday and helped Ian finish the job with winter fast approaching. The job would have taken Ian well into the New Year to finish. Another job well done by the lads. They worked hard and enjoyed it and I am always so proud of them when I see the finished project.

It is fair to say they did an absolutely fantastic job up there. They and their families can be proud of their efforts. That was also the general feeling amongst everyone who visited or saw their work. They did really help to transform Burn O'Vat. We got great acclaim for that work and rightly so. We got numerous letters from the Nature Conservatory Council thanking us for the work we did.

Here is one of them, with a request for further assistance:

Dear Sir,

I am warden of the Muir of Dinnet National Nature Reserve. The reason why I write is to ask if it would be possible for Bryan Glennie and a team of prisoners to come here and assist us with further work on the Burn O'Vat footpath sometime in April or May?

As you are well aware Bryan has brought teams out for a number of years. They have done some excellent work which is gratefully appreciated by us but more importantly by the large number of visitors who use the path each year.

If permission is granted there will be no cost to the prison authorities. All transport and material costs will be met by the Nature Conservancy Council.

I look forward to hearing from you and hopefully to having Bryan and the boys working with us again.

Yours sincerely Jim Parkin (park warden).

We also got a lot of positive publicity for our work in the local and even the national press.

The walkways are still there, though. I think some bits of it could be doing with getting replaced. One of my friends was up there lately and told me it is time the prisoners paid another visit, but I joked I don't think there is any chance of that happening now!

23

Life's a Beach in Balmedie

We got so much positive publicity from our efforts at Burn O'Vat that we received several more approaches for work and assistance from various projects across the North-east. Burn O'Vat was a great feather in the cap of HMP Aberdeen and to the inmates themselves because it showed the quality of work they produced. It was great that all their efforts hadn't gone unnoticed.

The Aberdeenshire councillor Paul Miller made an approach in 1989. He made his pitch on behalf of the 'Keep Grampian Beautiful' campaign. It was launched to clean up the area, as the region, disappointingly, was voted one of the worst in the United Kingdom. The local council wanted to turn things around and came up with this local campaign that was insti-gated to educate and change habits and to make Grampian a place to be proud of. Several projects were put in place to raise the profile and to generally tidy up the area.

Balmedie was part of Councillor Miller's constituency and he and the local people in the village expressed their growing concerns about the mess of Balmedie beach. It had always been a very popular beach with locals, sun worshippers and even walkers.

The problem was that over the winter months it wasn't quite so appealing, with all the debris and rubbish that had washed ashore from the shipping and oil industries.

Councillor Miller came to us and asked if we could provide some prisoners and staff to do a bit of a clean-up operation. They wanted us to tidy the beach up and to get it ready for the main summer season. We agreed because we knew the 'Keep Grampian Tidy' campaign was very high profile and we knew that once again the community would benefit from our work.

So we got the green light from the governor and then Councillor Miller took care of everything else. He put the facilities we needed in place. He left us a little caravan to have a seat, lunch, a cup of tea or to use the facilities. He also got the council to provide skips for the refuse collections so we could get rid of all the rubbish we weren't able to dispose of ourselves.

We cleaned up everything. Everything that was flammable was burnt. We would wait until the tide went out and then we would burn everything. The tide would then come in and wash the remains away. The rest was thrown into a giant skip. It was nothing like the recycling today. The rubbish and debris that was washed ashore was jaw-dropping, especially in the height of winter when the tides were higher.

Some of the debris that was washed up at Balmedie, if you pardon the pun, was absolutely criminal. We found a fridge and even a bed frame – the sort of stuff that should have been put to a refuge tip.

Some of the rubbish was that bad we struggled to move it by sheer brute force. We had to get hold of a local farmer and ask him to lend us his tractor and cart in order to get some things moved. That shows the size of the problem we were facing.

Another big problem along the ten-mile strip from Bridge of Don to Newburgh was from the offshore or more traditional North-east industries. There is no questioning the money and jobs that fishing and the old industry have brought to the area but in those early years they also caused a lot of damage to the environment. A big issue along the Balmedie beach stretch was oil drums. There were dozens and dozens of them that would be washed ashore. They came off ships and the oil rigs and goodness knows what sort of damage and pollution they caused. I shudder to think. Another problem was the fish boxes from the trawlers. They left a terrible mess with the wooden and plastic boxes. Thankfully the whole set-up is a lot greener today.

You also had the everyday waste that comes from visiting the beach. The number of glass and plastic bottles was amazing. If we'd known waste was so profitable, as it is today, we could have made the prison a fortune by recycling it all. It is fair to say there wasn't the same awareness of waste back then, but at least things have now changed for the better.

It wasn't just the clean-up side of things; there was also the safety element to the public as well. Some of the stuff the prisoners picked up, from broken glass to planks with rusty nails sticking out, could have done some real damage, especially to young children or babies playing innocently in the sand.

There were the obvious benefits from our work but it is fair to say the prisoners also got something back and felt they were doing something worthwhile.

I remember one of the prisoners we took out. He was serving a life sentence. It was the first time he had stepped outside of the prison in the fifteen years since he had been sent down. This was a hardened criminal but he was nearly in tears. He was so emotional. I don't think he had expected to be outside the prison walls again!

We were having a cup of tea and I remember him just looking out from the door of the caravan. He was just staring at everything, from the sand dunes to the sea, in total dismay. He probably thought he would never see outside of the prison walls again. It was great witnessing the prisoners' reactions and you could see this sort of project was a real positive – a shot in the arm to those lucky enough to be involved. We went and did regular clean-ups at Balmedie beach between 1989 and 1991.

We received more good headlines and publicity from Balmedie Beach. We helped to turn it into a top beach that people could visit all year round and it also proved a winner for the 'Keep Grampian Beautiful' campaign.

Councillor Paul Miller paid tribute to the prisoners and the team who did all the work at Balmedie. He said at the time 'The prisoners have done some very good work for the North-east public. This is a very good example from the inmates, it does good all round – from the workers to the public using the beach.'

24

DOWN ON THE BOARDWALK

Aberdeen District Council was next to get in touch with Craiginches after seeing the work and the impact the endeavours of our prisoners had made at Balmedie and at Burn O'Vat.

The council had initiated a joint project with the Nature Conservancy Council and the oil giants Texaco. That was in 1991. They had teamed up together to try and give something back to local communities. At that time the perception amongst many was that oil companies were only interested in making money and weren't really that interested in anything else.

We then had all these negative stories of what oil and gas was doing to the environment and the oil giants knew they had to clean up their acts and had to be seen to be cleaner and greener.

This was one of these good news projects, where Texaco worked in tandem with the Nature Conservancy Council. The council suggested places or areas that needed some work or investment and with Texaco's financial backing they would be able to transform certain areas.

Both parties also felt we could play a major part in one

of their landmark projects in Aberdeen. They wanted us to combine the skills we had used on both projects to tidy up the area around the mouth of the River Don, at the Bridge of Don, and to allow it to be designated as a local nature reserve.

The area is a popular site for walkers and families but it wasn't without its hazards. People would park their cars and come down from beside the Donmouth pub for a stroll or to walk their dogs. It was quite a drop and people were basically walking straight on to giant sand dunes. It was far from safe, especially as the dunes started to erode. It was also near impossible if you wanted wheelchair access to get down on to the beach.

The council had various complaints and knew they had to address the problem. The last thing they wanted was to leave themselves open to a claim against any potential injury. They also knew that any new work would really add to the area and help them attract more people to the beachfront.

The project officer for Aberdeenshire City Council, Judith Cox, coordinated with us and told us exactly what they were looking for. The council felt the best option was to put in wooden walkways like the ones that had been such a big success up at Burn O'Vat. We were to build steps and ramps at various points for wheelchair access.

The plan was to lay the walkways on either side of the River Don. The first walkway went from the Bridge of Don right down to the mouth of the river and the other ran parallel, leading straight on to the beach boulevard. We also had to put a ramp and steps in at the Donmouth on the other side of the river to maximise the access and to take out the massive drop down on to the sand. The second part of the walkway was laid the following year in 1992.

We got a group of four prisoners out again to put in the hard graft and within a couple of weeks we had laid and built the walkways, which ran to more than 400 metres.

We completely transformed the area in about two weeks. I knew what a shift the prisoners had put in but even I was surprised at how quickly they got the job done and to their usual immaculate standards.

We also got plenty of plaudits in the press, including some live footage on the television evening news show *North Tonight*. Texaco also filmed an entire day's work with the prisoners for their own promotional purposes. The council was delighted but the real achievement was seeing the buzz and excitement of the patients from Woodend Hospital as they were pushed along the riverside.

After we had completed the project we took some patients from Aberdeen's City Hospital, who were confined to wheelchairs, down to the Donmouth walkways. We let some of the prisoners take them for a walk along them. They loved being able to go along the Don, taking in the views and watching the goings-on in and around the neighbouring nature reserve. It was something new, as there had been no chance of getting a wheelchair down on the dunes before that. We saw at first hand the positive impact of the work. Seeing that was a great moment for the prisoners and myself because we were doing these projects to help others. To see them getting such enjoyment out of our work made it all worthwhile.

The prison governor, Bill Rattray, got a lovely letter from Aberdeen City Council thanking us for the work we had done with the boardwalks at the Donmouth. Bert Allen from Aberdeen City Council also came out to see us at the Donmouth, but we had actually completed our work a couple of hours earlier.

His thank you letter to the prisoner governor said:

I write to express my thanks to the Prison Service and in particular to Mr Bryan Glennie and his team for building the boardwalk at

Donmouth. I am very impressed by all that has been done and by the quality of the workmanship. The boardwalks have already attracted favourable comments from members of the public and I am sure the community, in particular disabled persons, will obtain a great deal of pleasure from the facilities which have been installed by the Prison Service.

I very much appreciate the level of cooperation with members of staff here in the department and I would hope that opportunities will arise in the not-so-distant future when we can work together again on environmental measures which will have lasting benefits and create further opportunities to enjoy the city and its natural setting.

I also received a letter from Chris Jackson, the principal planning officer, thanking me for my personal involvement. It said:

The City Council planning committee has now taken the final steps towards designation of Donmouth as a Local Nature Reserve and has instructed me to convey their thanks to all those involved in the project.

The planning and construction of the timber boardwalk carried out by yourself and the prisoners has been instrumental in improving access to the dunes, particularly for the less able. They have also considerably reduced erosion of these areas and the dune grasses are now re-establishing underneath and along the boardwalk. This project has been very worthwhile and has contributed towards the enhancement of an area which will be a valuable resource for Aberdeen.

'I would be grateful if you could pass on my thanks to the prisoners who I am sure can be proud of the work which they carried out to such a high standard under your supervision.

It was a nice touch and fitting tribute to the prisoners and their work. The fact that Donmouth is now a protected local nature reserve is also great to see. HMP Aberdeen could look proudly on, knowing we helped play our part. What more could we have asked for?

The Scottish Prison Service also got wind of the impact of our work. They had obviously given it the green light and had been kept abreast of things through the daily newspaper cuttings library. They sent a letter to the governor, Mr. Rattray. It was entitled: Donmouth Project and read:

Mr Glennie's initiative and commitment is, yet again, to be highly commended and I would wish to do so on behalf of the Scottish Prison Service.

This kind of community venture attracts nothing but the highest praise and credit both for the establishment and for the Service. It will also give me great pleasure to include this project in the Scottish Prison Service's annual report.

Perhaps you would also be kind enough to pass a copy of this letter on to Mr Glennie.

Alan Walker (Deputy Director of Operations)

25

There Has Been a Robbery

Theft and robbery are two of the crimes which could well have led to you serving time at HMP Aberdeen. We just didn't expect our inmates to become the victims!

It all centred round a local project in Torry which we got involved in in June/July 1992, doing some more outside work with the prisoners in association with Aberdeen City Council. This time it was for their 'Clean and Green' campaign. They worked on numerous regeneration projects all over the Granite City to tidy places up and to encourage more people to visit them.

The council asked if we could supply prisoners to aid a project right on our own doorstep. They wanted to give the walkway along the River Dee at Torry a bit of a clean and spruce up. It had been left untouched for years and needed a bit of manual work to be done on it such as cutting back trees and bushes to make it a bit more appealing for people to walk along.

In all honestly it had become a bit of an eyesore and at some points it was even bordering on the dangerous. The council wanted the majority of the work to be done around the Victoria Bridge area. They wanted to improve its existing walkways. They were keen to make it more accessible for all, offering wheelchair and pushchair access from the bridge all the way up to the fish houses at the opposite end.

The wooden walkways we built certainly made the area more accessible for the public and wheelchair users at the entrances beside the Victoria and Queen Elizabeth bridges. Our work cleaned up the area and made it a lot more appealing for the locals and visitors to use. It took a lot of hard graft from the prisoners over the space of several weeks. The project was another great success and made Torry a bit more appealing and obviously opened things up for a lot more people and families of all ages to visit.

We also thought it would be a good idea to finish things off by putting a bench along the walkway. We felt it would be good for walkers to have a quick seat or just to sit and relax on the riverside. It wasn't part of our remit but we thought it would be a worthwhile addition and would set things off nicely.

Having the joiner's workshop, and with so many skilled joiners amongst our inmates, meant that it wasn't going to be too difficult to get our hands on a sturdy wooden bench.

We spoke to George Hunter, the boss in the joiner's workshop, because bench-making was one of his many specialities and he had made dozens throughout the years.

The fact that it was for a local cause and was something for the surrounding community also whetted the appetite of George and his prisoners.

Within a few days we had a heavy-duty timber bench fully varnished and ready to be carried out on to the walkway. Once again, there could have been no complaints about the quality of work the men had produced. The bench was certainly made to last!

We put the bench along the walkway, looking across the

river over to the esplanade. We thought it would be nice for people and visitors just to sit there in such a picturesque location. Afterwards, we looked proudly at it knowing that we were able to sign off because our work on another project was done. Or so we thought!

A member of staff was out for his walk the next day at lunchtime and as they came along the walkway and they noticed the bench had disappeared. It had been stolen! We couldn't believe it. Who would want to steal a bench? Something that had been put there to benefit the whole community!

You just wonder about some people. There are some unscrupulous individuals who would steal anything. That is the sad reality of the world we live in.

The local newspapers ran some articles to help us try and find the missing bench. We got some decent headlines and coverage but we never did manage to locate it.

I was absolutely livid at the time. I was quoted as saying: 'It is very sad. We have been doing a lot of work for this project. The riverside is right on our doorstep and a lot of the prisoners had jumped at the chance to work for their local community.' Even Aberdeen City Council got involved. Their environmental officer George Duffus added: 'These benches were not for the council they were for the people of Aberdeen. It is sickening.' Thankfully, there are more good people around in Aberdeen.

We went back to the joiner's workshop and told George Hunter and the boys what had happened. They were as bemused and as angry as us.

If we had caught the thief and thrown him into Craiginches, I dread to think what would have happened!

George and the rest of his team in the joiner's workshop immediately told us they would make us another bench, which they did. We then took it back out and put it in the same location as before. This time we had learned from our mistakes. We bolted the bench down and if anyone wanted to take it then they were going to need to take the riverbank with them! This time the bench was there for the long haul.

The riverside project was another massive hit and was testament to the prisoners again. It proved to be another popular project and that was seen with the number of people who used the walkway or would be sitting on the bench looking across the water. That was where the real joy and sense of fulfilment came from everyone involved in these projects. When I think about the bench being stolen now, it is quite funny, but back then it was no laughing matter.

26

Woodend Hospital

We had good links with Aberdeen Royal Infirmary and Woodend Hospital. We had done a string of fund-raisers for different wards. We had also been up and done various events in and around the hospital.

This time we took on a project at Ward 19 at Woodend. It was a twenty-five-bed ward for females awaiting geriatric assessment. We had already been up to the ward and had done a prison slide show to entertain some of their patients one afternoon. We were showing and telling the people at the hospital some of the things we did. Fiona Thomson, the voluntary services coordinator for Woodend and Morningfield Hospitals, got in touch and said they could do with a hand in gutting out the ward.

We had raised money for various wards and causes at the hospital but in 1994 we decided to go one step further and the Aberdeen Prison Community Links Committee adopted the ward for the year. The four-man committee met with the sister of the ward and the voluntary coordinator at the hospital to see where we could help in and around the ward.

When we first set foot in Ward 19, we all agreed that it had seen better days and was in dire need of being brightened up. It was quite tired and dark and was hardly inspiring for the patients who had to spend a lot of their time there.

So the first step was to get funds so the ward could be decorated.

We raised money through the usual avenues: street collections, football sweeper cards, the sale of prison merchandise. We also held regular jumble sales in the church hall at Torry and did regular coffee mornings, where Mrs Aitken would supply us with rolls and cakes, while Ian Law our local shopkeeper beside the prison would give us loads of sugar, milk, tea bags and coffee. Every year we had different charities and that particular year was Woodend.

There were also bingo afternoons in the ward run by prison staff, which the patients enjoyed. One of the main events for Ward 19 was a sponsored hill walk. Hospital and prison staff along with friends walked from Braemar to Blairgowrie, which was an impressive total of around twenty-seven miles and raised a lot of money.

The ward was painted by the hospital staff from top to bottom. We then got new furniture, including a new three-piece suite for the day room and we also bought some much-needed new dinner sets as well. We also brought in some plants and hanging baskets to try and make the ward look a bit more homely.

The prison also got on well with *Aberdeen Journals*. I knew their managing director Alan Scott well and when he heard about the work we were doing for Ward 19 he also wanted to get involved. Alan arranged for a number of old photographs from in and around Aberdeen to be printed off and then got them framed so we could hang them on the walls of the ward just to finish things off. It was a nice touch and one I know the staff and patients really appreciated because the number of comments we got about the photographs was unbelievable.

To finish off that project we took the patients from the ward down to the Duthie Park, with the four prisoners being the escorts for the afternoon. We took them for tea and coffee and a walk around the Winter Gardens and just had a good laugh. The patients and prisoners really enjoyed the afternoon.

This was the lovely thank you note we received:

To the Aberdeen Prison Community Links Committee,

Thank you to the committee for volunteering to adopt a ward at Woodend hospital for the twelve-month period from January 1994.

The ward selected was Ward 19, which is a twenty-five-bedded female geriatric assessment ward. An initial meeting was held between the four members of the committee, the ward sister and myself to establish how funds raised could be effectively spent for the benefit of patients and appropriate social activities could be arranged.

It was felt in the first instance that the ward environment needed brightening up so the committee provided hanging baskets and plants for the corridor, a selection of pictures, five dinner sets, a three-piece suite all of which created a more homely atmosphere in the day room.

Regarding social involvement, the committee organised a bingo evening in the ward and with the help of four prisoners as escorts, they gave a group of patients a tour round local Winter Gardens followed by afternoon tea.

Over the past months one prisoner has made visits to the ward to chat to patients, some of whom who have had few visitors of their own and do enjoy a bit of company.

As well as the committee, other members of the prison service have been involved in supporting the project by participating in fund-raising events, etc. Money has been raised through activities organised by the committee which include a football sweep and the sale of goods with the Community Links logo. There was also a sponsored hill walk which ward staff, prison staff and friends participated in.

An excellent rapport has been built up between ward staff, the committee, prisoners and the patients. Great improvements have also been made to the ward environment and to the patients' quality of life during their hospital stay which has been greatly enhanced by the involvement of the Community Links, which is without doubt worthy of recognition.

Fiona Thomson.
Voluntary Services Coordinator of City Hospitals in Aberdeen.

27

Aberdeen Royal Infirmary Bowled Over by Craiginches

I bowled at the Aberdeen Royal Infirmary Bowling Club. The club was within the grounds of the hospital. I became a member and bowled there for a number of years. The committee knew that I worked at HMP Aberdeen and were also aware that I had, along with some of our prisoners, assisted with various projects out and about from Burn O'Vat to Balmedie and Bridge of Don.

The committee, via our then president, Tom Cowe, approached me to ask if there was any possibility we could get the prisoners to help at the bowling club. They wanted some heavy duty maintenance done at the club. They needed the ditch round the green dug out because heavy rain had caused serious damage to it.

They required us to barrow in all the replacement blocks for two of the members who were going to come in and build the new wall.

Tom made the plea for help from the prison because they were stuck in a bit of a catch-22 situation. He explained that at the time in the local press. Tom said: 'Most of our younger members work all day and we don't have enough money to employ an outside contractor, so we asked for the prison's help.' It was one that I couldn't really say no to, although the final clearance still had to come from the governor, Scott Ogilvie. Just as well it wasn't a problem. I was given the go-ahead and assured of my ARI Bowling Club membership for a few more years!

I then went back to the prison to get three prisoners for the job. For these projects we picked those who had achieved a trustee status and were often nearing the end of their sentences, although in fairness I wasn't short of volunteers to work on this project. We had a few keen bowlers, others who were just sporty and some prisoners who just wanted the chance to work outside the prison. I picked a trio who I knew would put in a real shift and could also cope with the physical demands of the job. I then took them down and we worked together under the supervision of the head green keeper Dougie Alexander. The guys all worked like Trojans and at one point I even had to tell them to slow down a bit because they were so full of enthusiasm and wanted to make the most of their few hours of freedom. The prisoners knew that if they impressed there would be more chance of getting asked on to future jobs.

We got all the work done at the bowling club over the space of four or five days, which saw the guys having to carry in more than 1,400 blocks. They were then cemented in by the two members, who, if I remember correctly, were skilled bricklayers. The newly built wall was then covered with AstroTurf, which was laid down right into the ditch.

We then gave the place a general tidy-up and got everything spick and span and ready for the new season. The committee really appreciated our efforts and so did my fellow members.

Some of the prisoners were also quoted in the local press

at the time. One said: 'We like the work as it teaches us a trade and skills we can use when we get out.' Another added: 'There should be a lot more of this because it gets us outside. It is very frustrating being banged up in prison the whole time!'

28

Impact of Such Projects

'From the minute inmates arrived they had their freedom taken away and had to play by our rules. It didn't mean we couldn't try to improve their quality of life and I think most prisoners appreciated what we tried to do.' - Bryan Glennie, *Evening Express*.

The outdoor projects were great for the prisoners. I believe more prisons should try and adopt similar projects because there are real benefits for the prison, the inmates and the community projects they work on.

It was never a problem finding prisoners who wanted to be involved. The biggest problem was picking the right ones. I would liaise with my fellow officers, mainly those who worked in the work sheds and in the halls, before I would decide who was going to go out that week or on a certain project that was coming up. As mentioned previously, those we picked had all achieved a more trusted status and were often near the end of their sentences. I would take recommendations from my fellow officers and from there we would decide on the three or four prisoners best suited for that particular job.

Once we had narrowed that down we would then get the

prisoners in and get their thoughts. Some maybe weren't interested but most would have bitten your hand off just to get out for a few hours of near freedom! Each inmate was told in no uncertain terms that if they wanted to be involved they had to adhere to our rules and if they stepped out of line then it was all over for them!

It didn't matter what they were doing time for, it didn't matter if it was a murderer or a petty thief, that didn't matter to me. What mattered to me was the fact that I felt I could trust them. I was happy with that. I worked on the beach with two inmates who were doing life and another who had been sentenced to fifteen years.

I would also name one of the prisoners as my foreman. I just thought it was a good idea because if somebody was leaning on another prisoner or putting an unnecessary strain on him then the foreman would know the score and would come and let me know. That way we were able to sort things out before they became a problem.

The only time I had any such problems was when we were working on the nature reserve at Bridge of Don. One of the prisoners had organised for his wife to come down and drop off some money for him. That, as you would expect, was totally taboo. I was sitting in the caravan having my lunch when I heard a commotion. I went outside and my foreman was having a debate with this other prisoner. I knew something was up because the guy who had started the argument was the foreman and somebody I got on really well with. I had worked with him for a number of years on projects. He was a genuine guy.

I sent them both into the caravan and asked them what had happened. The foreman explained how this other prisoner had tried to hatch this plan for his wife to come down and give him money. So right away I went on to the radio and got a van sent out to get the other guy back behind the prison gates before anything else could happen. The next day we returned to the Bridge of Don but with only three prisoners and from that day onwards the other prisoner didn't get another day trip again! That was the one and only occasion I had anything like that in my time with the Scottish Prison Service.

There was an inmate who came down from HMP Peterhead. He had served fifteen years up there before he came down to Craiginches. Some of the bosses knew there were a few projects coming up and they said to me: 'Why don't you give him a chance?' I agreed and the first project he came out with me on was at the bowling club at the Aberdeen Royal Infirmary. He took to it like a duck to water and just absolutely loved it. He then came out and helped me three or four times cleaning up Balmedie beach. He then moved on and eventually was downgraded again to an open prison, so that shows how some prisoners can change and be reformed.

One of the life-serving prisoners was part of one of the projects but I noticed a problem with him one night. He was on a diet at that time. Prisoners who had special dietary needs had to go through to the prison kitchen to get their food first, before the rest of the inmates. There were always staff stationed at different points in the corridor on the way to the dining room. I was there when I saw him come back through and I could see he was far from happy. As he was heading back towards the dining room I knew something wasn't quite right so I stopped him and asked what was wrong. We had a good relationship, thanks to our work together through our outside projects and so I felt I could speak to him. He just turned and said: 'That bastard is not speaking to me like that!' I looked down and saw he had his plastic dinner knife in his hand. He was on his way back to the dining room to have a go at a prisoner who had served him his dinner. He had said something and left us with a potential issue. I just warned him that if he went ahead with his threat there wouldn't be any more project work outside of the prison.

We had just finished the Balmedie project and there was word in the pipeline that we were going to start work at the bowling green at Aberdeen Royal Infirmary. I just told him: 'Do yourself a favour and get back to your cell. You enjoyed Balmedie beach, didn't you? The bowling green is coming up soon and if you go through there with the knife then you can forget that or any other future projects!' He quickly took stock of the situation, nodded his head in agreement and then headed back through to his cell in A Hall. Thankfully that was the end of the matter, the prisoner didn't take things any further and he was able to join us on future projects. Yet he could have thrown that all away for a few seconds of madness!

That incident, however, showed how important these projects were to the prisoners and played their part in keeping some of them on the straight and narrow.

THE CHARITABLE
WING

29

DEDICATED TO OUR DOUGLAS

Good causes were always a big thing at Her Majesty's Prison Aberdeen. The project that got the ball rolling was without doubt the one that was closest to our hearts and touched our lives more so than any of the others. It all came from our efforts to raise money in memory of our friend and former colleague Douglas Ruxton – the very man who had helped me to take my first steps into the prison service.

Dougie died in 1984 after a brave battle with leukaemia. Our initial fund-raising efforts in his name led to the charitable arm of the prison being set up.

Dougie was a really popular member of staff at Craiginches and beyond. I knew him well as we were both Insch boys. As mentioned earlier, he had been heavily influential in me joining the prison service and when I started I also worked closely with him.

I was put in the second division and Douglas was like a mentor in those early weeks and months. He was more of a guiding hand, as he was already an established member of staff. He was such a lovely person and member of the team. He was well liked. When it was confirmed that Dougie had leukaemia it was a real hammer-blow to us all. We all knew what a strong and determined character he was and we all hoped and prayed that he would come through the other side. Sadly, it wasn't to be. It was a real shame.

We remained close friends right up until the end. I used to go up and see him when he was lying in the hospital. It really was heartbreaking. It was so sickening, the decline in Dougie's condition. When he did pass away it turned out to be a blessing in disguise. He had been in so much pain and was a shadow of the man we knew and loved. It was a real set-back to all the staff at Craiginches. He was a massive loss because he was such a popular colleague and friend.

Some of my fellow staff came to me and said they would like to do something in Dougie's honour. I don't know why they came to me, maybe it was because they knew I was close to him. I was really taken aback by the real desire to do something in his name. Just about every member of staff wanted to get involved and play their part.

I knew then there was no holding us back but I still thought it was best to get in touch with his wife before we decided to do anything. I knew things were still raw for her and the family, as it was with us friends, and we certainly didn't want to do anything that would upset her or that she didn't want us to do.

I went to visit Isma and explained how the staff at Craiginches all wanted to do something in honour of Dougie. I asked her if she had any ideas as to what she would like us to do. She said she would get in contact with Dr Audrey Dawson, who was his doctor at Aberdeen Royal Infirmary. She said she would speak with her and then come back to me.

Isma got back in touch and said it would be a great gesture in Dougie's name and, if possible, she would like us to raise money for Ward 47 at Aberdeen Royal Infirmary. It was the leukaemia ward where Dougie had spent a lot of time in his last few months with us.

Dougie and Isma always spoke highly of the staff and the work they did for him while he was in getting his treatment. So we thought it would be good to give them something back and at the same time pay our own more lasting tribute to him.

We got in touch with the staff on Ward 47 to find out where they felt any money raised could be best used. They came back and confirmed that a computer system and terminal for the ward would really help them and their administration. It seemed really basic at the time but most of their archive records and work was still done manually on cards and files. It wasn't so much the work but it was the time it took. The staff felt that a new computer system would free up more time for the staff to deal with more important tasks, like caring for the patients and offering support to their families.

We got prices for the equipment and we were told it would cost around £2,000. So that was what we set for our original target for the Douglas Ruxton memorial fund.

We held sponsored walks and even a sponsored slim for those who were looking to lose a few inches. We also organised a jumble sale, a dance night and several other different competitions. As a finale we held a dinner dance in the Old King's Highway in Aberdeen.

It wasn't much of a surprise that our original target was quickly smashed. That was down to the popularity of Dougie.

We ended up more than doubling our original target and finished on an impressive £5,200, which was a lot of money back in the mid-1980s.

It allowed the ward to not only buy their computer equipment but to extend some of the other facilities they offered on the ward.

We were also delighted that Isma agreed to come up to Ward 47 to hand over the new equipment. It was quite an emotional day for all concerned. We had all put a lot of work into things and wanted to do him and the Ruxton family proud. I think everyone at Craiginches did that to honour the name of our long lost friend, Douglas Ruxton.

It was emotional but there was such an enthusiasm to do Dougie and his name proud. I think we can all say we did. The hospital and his family were all delighted. It was the least we could have done for Dougie, who had touched all our lives.

30

CRAIGINCHES SHOWS ITS HEART

Raising the money for Douglas Ruxton proved only to be the start. From there things snowballed. We realised we could do a lot more for the community and the less needy via the prison. What we raised in honour of Dougie showed what could be done and achieved. It was also another positive aspect of our work at Her Majesty's Prison Aberdeen.

I knew it was a big job to manage these sorts of projects so I thought it would be better to get quite a few people involved. Initially I roped in Allan Grant, Ernie Christie and Allan MacKinnon and what a decision that turned out to be – we were a brilliant team and worked so well together. We decided to call ourselves the Aberdeen Prison Community Links Project, which basically became the charitable wing of the prison in 1988. Many years later in the middle of 2014, with only three members left on our committee, we got together again to arrange a reunion for retired staff members which you can read about later in the book. It was a great success and showed we still had all our organising skills for such events.

Our initial idea was to go out into the community and to promote the prison and the work we did. It was more a sort of press relations exercise at first, trying to raise our profile in and around the various parts of Aberdeen. The move was initially thought out by the committee, so we then approached our prison governor to see what his thoughts were on our idea. He thought it would be a good idea because the prison and the outside community were very much kept apart. There was very little interaction – it was pretty much us and them. Nobody knew what we did other than hold prisoners.

We knew there was a lot more going on and we wanted to make people aware of it. So our initial idea was to put together a slide show of life and our work in the prison.

The governor bought us a camera and we then went round the prison taking photographs of various things so we could give people an insight into what life was like behind bars. We didn't take photographs of prisoners because that would have been a breach of their human rights but we were able to show different parts of the prison and the workshops and empty cells.

We started by going out and speaking to groups in and around the city but things just escalated out of hand. We ended up going out two or three times a week and could have been anywhere across Aberdeen or the surrounding North-east, even as far out as Ballater or my hometown of Insch. We needed a few of us just to cope with the demand.

We also wanted to try and promote what we were doing and make it a bit more visual. So we came up with a logo for the Craiginches Community Links. The logo was of a cartoon prisoner sitting in a corner with a ball and chain round his ankle. It was the brainchild of Allan Grant and one of the prisoners – as always we wanted them to have their input into things if it was possible.

We then got the logo on tiepins, T-shirts, tea towels, sweaters, badges and pens. We would never ask for money

My days as an amateur boxing referee.

Soccer stars face questions at Craiginches

■ Dons trio (from left) Robert Connor, Craig Robertson and Jim Bett arrive at Craiginches Prison with principal prison officer Mr Gus Gill.

The three soccer stars were appearing in front of one of their smallest crowds of the season last night.

They appeared in the jail's chapel to answer questions from about 30 inmates.

Some of the questions were sharp and the answers equally so. The trio had given up their free evening for the experience of being in prison — as guests of the governor.

Robert said: "I found it a very interesting experience and there were enough good questions to keep us all busy talking. I just hope the lads enjoyed it. I certainly did."

Jim said: "It's certainly nice to visit the men inside and try and let them forget their troubles for a short while. It's also nice to know you are coming out the same night!"

Craig Robertson, the "new boy" among the three Dons, said: "I didn't expect to be in prison so soon after coming to Aberdeen and I must say it was nice to be asked. It's the only way to do it."

Three Aberdeen FC players, Robert Connor, Craig Robertson and Jim Bett, arriving at the prison for a question and answer session with the inmates.

Toyah Wilcox, with members of her band and myself,
after she performed a concert for the prisoners.

The completed Ward 19 decorated with pictures of Aberdeen and hanging baskets.

One of the finished walkways we built at the nature reserve at Donmouth.

The Community Links Committee at the launch of the logo. Allan Grant, myself, Allan MacKinnon and Ernie Christie with volunteer Charlotte Leys.

Allan MacKinnon, Charlotte Leys and myself receiving the Scottish Employee in the Community award at the Grangemouth Oil Refinery.

Myself with my Butler Trust award presented by The Princess Royal at Lambeth Palace, London.

The Princess Royal,
with myself and
governor
Mr W. Rattray, on her
visit to the prison.

The Princess Royal unveiling the plaque at the gate
entrance along with governor Mr W. Rattray.

A photo of the Black Maria as we found it in the farm yard.

The Black Maria loaded on a trailer for the journey back to Craiginches.

The Black Maria starting out on the Centenary Parade
from the Castlegate Aberdeen to the prison.

Ernie Christie, Allan Grant and myself receiving the British Employee
in the Community award at the BAFTA building in London.

Four staff members from Craiginches prison picked to represent
the SPS Bowling Association against England in Rugby.

REUNION: Retired prison officers from a former city jail have held a reunion dinner in Aberdeen. Around 65 retired employees from Craiginches Prison in Torry attended. Organiser Bryan Glennie said: "The event was absolutely brilliant."

The reunion in 2015 of retired staff that had worked
at Craiginches during their careers.

for the slide shows but we would put out some merchandise after it that people would buy and help us to boost our funds. So we would always get plenty of sales.

It was strange because word certainly got around and we ended up sending stuff as far afield as Spain and even America. It showed things were really taking off.

The slide shows remained a central strand of our work. After each showing we would hold question and answer sessions and they proved very popular. We would visit anywhere from schools and community centres to the Women's Rural Institute and church groups. The feedback was unbelievable.

I remember we held a similar event for the Rotary Club in a hotel in Dyce. I actually met up with one of my old teachers from Insch school, Gordon Brewster. Gordon did the acknowledgements at the end and thanked us on behalf of the Rotary Club and their guests. I joked that this was only a set-up but he said no, it meant a lot to the Rotary Club and they had got some really good feedback from its members.

So much so I was asked to go and do the same presentation for the Rotary Club in the Bridge of Don the next week. Gordon turned up and I joked: 'Are you stalking me? What are you doing here?' He replied: 'There was so much going on last week in Dyce I couldn't take it all in and I asked if I could come across to the Bridge of Don to watch it again.'

The Rotary Club proved to be a real ally to the Links Committee. The Dyce branch actually gave us a sizeable donation to go towards our chosen charities because their members had voted us their best talk and presentation of that year. That was a great honour in itself for the committee and showed we were, at least, doing something right.

Things at the prison were very much a team affair but away from work we also had to rely on the support of our families. Our hours, at times, were unsociable and doing extra work outside of shifts, as we did, meant we spent even less time at home. So we thought we would arrange a prison night for our partners and our families. It would be best to organise such events for a Sunday evening when the prison was locked up for the night. It allowed those closest and dearest to us to see the environment in which we worked and gave them more of an insight into the prison, rather than hearing and visualising everything second-hand. I think the families enjoyed it and it was all part of opening the prisons door that little bit wider. There was a great response from our nearest and dearest. We decided that because of the numbers involved we would split the groups up and have a couple of evening visits. On each night we split the groups into twelve to take them round the inner sanctum of Craiginches.

John Watt was the principal officer on duty for the visits and took some of our esteemed visitors around our workplace.

John said: 'We decided to invite the wives along to see the environment in which the staff has to work. We thought it would help them to understand the strains and pressures which the staff had to put up with and may have helped them to realise why their partners reacted in certain ways away from work.

'When we held the visit it was the first of its type at Aberdeen although Barlinnie prison, in Glasgow, had held a similar event a few years earlier.'

It proved a useful project, as I know it gave some of our wives and partners a real insight and also opened a few eyes just to what the staff had to work through on a daily basis. I think it worked for both sides and also made our families even more a part of the team.

The committee regularly got together to consider various approaches for help from various charities.

We raised money at the prison all the time. We had a correct score competition every week and we always had money to fund various things.

Every year as part of our annual fund-raisers we held a jumble sale and coffee morning in the local church hall in Torry. All the staff contributed to this, with a special thanks to Aitkens Bakery and our local corner shop beside the prison, which was run by Ian Law, who made huge contributions to these events. Some people would even just go to the coffee mornings just because we had Aitkens rolls. That was even before they had got the royal seal of approval! This helped swell the coffers for some wonderfully good causes.

31

Good Causes

CLAN

Charlotte Leys came in and volunteered for us at the prison. She would make the tea and coffee for the visitors when they came up. She was heavily involved with CLAN (Cancer Link Aberdeen and North). CLAN is a very worthwhile charity that is still going from strength to strength in Aberdeen. They offer help to cancer suffers of all ages and provide help and support for patients, families and their friends every step of the way. They provide an invaluable service and cover the whole of Aberdeen with patients in the islands of Orkney and Shetland.

Charlotte approached us, as CLAN was looking to try and raise significant funds. They wanted to get enough money behind them to build their own purpose-built cancer facility, or CLAN House, as they wanted to call it. Their premises had initially been based in Justice Mill Lane in Aberdeen city centre. Their building had seen better days and wasn't really suited to what their patients really needed, but at that point it was more a case of make do and mend, with all their monies going to make the lives of cancer sufferers and their families that bit easier.

CLAN launched their buy-a-brick campaign to coincide with the charity's own tenth birthday. They had set their initial target at £500,000 with the one aim to be able to buy and build the facility they and their patients so desperately craved.

When raising money for CLAN was put to the committee it was fair to say it sailed through unopposed. It was given a resounding yes, knowing the impact it had and would make on so many of our lives.

We did various different things to raise money for CLAN. One of the fund-raisers we did was to take out a stall at the outdoor Aberdeen Christmas Fayre. The event used to see Union Street closed and pedestrianised so people could walk up and down the market stalls. It sadly has now been surpassed by the International Christmas Market which has lots of overseas foods, delicacies and sweets sold, with a few added extras like giant fairground rides.

It is fair to say things are a lot grander today. Back then we took a basic stall from which we would sell our T-shirts, tiepins and pens. They all had the Community Links logo on them so not only were we making money for good causes we were also raising awareness into the bargain.

We also had other different attractions like a tombola and we sold clothing and merchandise.

We raised more than £600 from our efforts at the Christmas Fayre. We presented CLAN with that initial cheque and got some very good newspaper coverage over it, with Allan MacKinnon from the committee seen handing the cheque over to CLAN coordinator Cathy Low in one of the photographs.

Our efforts were applauded but every single person on the committee thought we could do that bit more. We felt there was still a bit of unfinished business. So we agreed to raise more money for CLAN through a never-ending list of fund-raising events we dreamed up at the prison.

There was also a Friends of CLAN group set up, independent of the prison, who were going to continually raise funds for the charity. We decided we could give them a helping hand and at their inaugural meeting we handed them over a cheque for £1,000.

The good thing was that CLAN continued to raise money and with the help of the North-east public were able to move into premises in Caroline Place in Aberdeen. It was still a long road in front if they wanted to build that purpose-built facility that had been the pipe dream with their buy-a-brick campaign.

That dream finally became a reality in October 2011 when CLAN House was officially opened at 120 Westburn Road, just a short walk from Aberdeen Royal Infirmary.

CLAN House now proudly offers specific areas for families and children, a wide range of therapies and outdoor space for visitors to enjoy, along with other health and well-being services.

It is good to see that everybody's good work and dedication has made it happen and that the prisoners and staff of Craiginches helped them take a small step on what has been a long but fruitful journey.

BUS PUSH FOR THE BLIND

The Royal National Institute of Blind People was another beneficiary of the Community Links Committee. We got involved with them through Stan Flett. Stan was partially sighted but was a very talented accordion player. He had his own band and played a number of gigs for us at Craiginches for the prisoners.

I also met Stan regularly in and about the city. He was

heavily involved with the RNIB. He would always keep me abreast of what they were up to and how they were looking to raise money.

I didn't say anything but the next time we had a committee meeting I decided to put the RNIB forward as a possible avenue for one of our future fund-raising ventures.

The RNIB got the support it needed from the committee and our next question was how were we going to try and raise the funds? Somebody then came up with the rather bizarre idea of a bus push between the prisoners and the staff. That really was something different and innovative, even by our standards. So we got in touch with the bus operator at the time, which was Grampian Transport, and asked if this was a feasible venture, especially as we needed their help. They were great; they came back and said no problem and they would give us the loan of a couple of buses. I did jokingly ask them if they would take the handbrake off before we got them, certainly for us if not the prisoners!

The next challenge was to find a suitable venue for our bus push and thankfully Grampian Transport stepped in to assist us again. They had links with the Aberdeen Exhibition and Conference Centre out at the Bridge of Don. That had a massive car parking area which was ideal for our needs – although I am sure that a bus push would never have come into the planners' thinking when the AECC was first built!

We got everything set up and transported the prisoners up to the AECC. I am certain a few of them had been putting plenty of work in at the gym before the big day.

Anyway, we did the first bus push. We split into our teams, so there were four officers and four prisoners competing against each other. It was a very competitive affair, with neither side wanting to lose. It is fair to say we came off second-best. The prisoners had the upper hand, so I remember we said it was the best of three to try and save face. We did win the second and took it to a third. It was all in the balance but to add insult to injury the prisoners came out on top in the decider. It was good for the inmates. It gave them a wee boost and bragging rights over the staff for a few days when we got back to the prison. It is a small thing but it gave the place a buzz, although maybe that was more for the prisoners than the staff!

OUR PRISON PICASSOS

One of the educational courses some of the inmates were attending was painting. The classes were twice a week and were held by Graham Swanson, who was a lecturer at Aberdeen College of Commerce. The group of six prisoners started off doing various paintings and then gradually worked themselves up to a real decent level. So much so that they decided they would donate them to Ward 8 in the Royal Aberdeen Children's Hospital.

They painted a number of different pictures on the theme of television cartoon characters. Garfield was one of the final portraits along with his dog, Odie. They were really, really good and the prisoners also put their own message – 'Goodnight kids' – on them. It was a really nice touch and, in fairness, the children loved them. Ward 8 was for children recovering from infectious diseases. I was quoted in the local press at the time saying: 'The prisoners really wanted to help the children and hopefully the pictures will cheer them up while they are recovering.' I think that proved to be more than the case.

THE *SUNDAY POST* QUIZ KINGS

A few members of the Craiginches staff, Allan Grant, Ernie Christie, Allan MacKinnon and Carol Bruce, got together to take on the weekly *Sunday Post* quiz for charity.

The iconic weekly Scottish newspaper challenge saw teams get together to answer twenty general knowledge questions. For every answer they got right £2.50 would go to the charity or charities of their choice.

The two groups chosen by our staff were Aberdeen Royal Children's Hospital Ward 4, and Ward 31 at Aberdeen Royal Infirmary.

The team had to submit their answers and they then appeared in the following weekend's *Sunday Post*, marked, along with the answers and picture portraits of the team. Having seen their head shots, it would have been hard to distinguish if they were criminals or prison officers. I think in the end their hats just gave them the benefit of the doubt.

They had questions of varying difficulty, for example: Name five kinds of pastry. Who was the manager of Liverpool Football Club before Kenny Dalglish? Who is the longest serving member on Coronation Street?

These were all answers that the team got right.

The questions they came unstuck on were: What's reckoned to be Britain's highest value car registration number? Who is the patron saint of tax men? And what word is a device used to muffle a trumpet and a swan?

Maybe it wasn't too much of a surprise they got them wrong!

The team did really well, in fairness, and got seventeen out of twenty, earning around £42.50 to both charities, which we topped up with some aid from the Community Links fund.

OPENING THE DOORS AND OFFERING CLEAN GETAWAY CARS

We held a half-open day at Craiginches. We opened the doors and let the public in to see what exactly went on at HMP Aberdeen. It wasn't quite access all areas because visitors couldn't get near the prison wings but they were given access to the front building and entrance areas.

We put on a slide show in the visitors' room, and tea and coffee was served up in the prison staff room, while outside we had staff and trusted prisoners on hand to make even more money by washing cars in the car park – to make sure everybody got a clean getaway. We quite literally cleaned up that day. All the money we raised went to leukaemia and kidney projects at Aberdeen Royal Infirmary.

We also did something similar when we held a slide show of our work in the prison and then followed it up with tea and coffee. Whilst visiting we washed the visitors' cars.

ENSURING IT WASN'T TORCHER FOR THE STUDENTS

The Torcher Parade is famous in Aberdeen. It is an event where students dress up and deck out lorries with displays and disguises. The parade then goes through the city and sees students collect donations from the watching public.

Most of the money is taken via student collection cans but one year they had forgotten to sort out the cans in advance. So, in a panic, they approached the prison to see if we would re-label their collection cans so they could get them ready in time. It was only a few days before the parade and they were really up against it. We got the prisoners involved and made the new labels and sealed the cans so the Torcher Parade could continue without a hitch. The students were delighted and from then on in came to us when it was time to re-label and use their cans.

SMELLING OF ROSES

We were approached by the world-famous Anderson's Roses, who were based in the city. They needed all their roses cut ahead of the Aberdeen Rose Festival. They asked if we could give them some prisoners to assist them. It was a big job and we ended up sending out around four prisoners at a time to their fields at Maryculter to pick and prune roses for them.

Anderson's were to give the flowers away at the festival and also wanted some of them to decorate the horse-drawn carriage for that year's Rose Queen. The artwork and flower arrangement for the carriage was made by the prisoners as well. Some of our prisoners may have had light fingers but that team was certainly green-fingered!

Anderson's also appreciated the prisoners' work and made a donation to the Community Links fund.

TORRY ARTS FESTIVAL

The Community Links Committee, as you will all now be aware, tried to involve the local people of Torry with the prison as much as we could. Torry organised its own arts festival and we felt it was only right to get involved. It was a week-long event and the organiser, Ron Slater, wanted to get some of the prisoners and Craiginches officers involved in the Torry Arts Festival.

So we started off by getting a football team together between the officers and the prisoners. We did a few weeks training and then we played a glamour friendly against a team from the Torry Youth Project. It was good because there was a fair bit of interaction.

We also had more than our fair share of budding artists and the festival arranged for a lot of the work to be publicly displayed at the Torry Urban Adventure Project, along with some drawings and photography from pupils at the local secondary school, Torry Academy.

There were also other events including arts and crafts, face painting, a quiz night, window painting, a darts competition, lace-making events and dance workshops.

The highlight of the festival was on the Saturday when there was a sailing regatta on the River Dee and it was followed by a large festival, where over seven bands played in Torry's Walker Park.

The festival was a massive success and not only raised the profile of Torry but brought thousands of people into the area over the space of that week. It was amazing because the Torry Arts Festival had kicked off initially as a one-day event and suddenly it was now running all week.

The good thing was that all the money raised from the week went to local independent groups and charities in Torry. So it was a win-win situation for all concerned.

A LUCKY UNICORN

Grampian Healthcare's Unicorn Enterprises was a project that helped patients who were recovering from mental illness. They had an employment assessment and rehabilitation centre just off Great Western Road in Aberdeen. The problem was that their premises were really dull and dingy. They weren't exactly open and welcoming and weren't what you wanted to walk into, especially if you felt a wee bit down yourself.

It was a big job because their building was quite big. Their problem was they didn't have much money because they were a charity and all the revenue streams they did have went directly to their patient services. So that was when they got in touch with the prison and asked if we could do the work for them.

They needed their building painted and generally cleaned up. We took three prisoners up and they did all the work for them over the course of a couple of weeks. We did that free of charge. Their building was simply in need of a makeover and we felt this was a group who genuinely needed our help.

We got press coverage for that project. I remember there was an article along with a photograph of the three prisoners on various steps on a ladder.

A spokeswoman for Unicorn was also quoted. She said: 'This has really been a mutually satisfying venture. We had wanted the place to be painted for a while. We had thought of asking the prisoners and we are delighted we did because their work has been brilliant.' That particular article also gave some of my prison colleagues and the rest of the committee a good laugh as I was renamed Brian Glinny in it. Thankfully, the name never stuck! Anyway Mr Glinny was equally as delighted with the prisoners as myself. 'These lads have been working like Trojans,' he claimed. 'This gives them a sense of responsibility towards the community. The patients have also enjoyed seeing some new faces around as well.' By the time all the work was done their premises were completely transformed. It was hard to believe it was the same building. Just a simple coat of paint and tidy up and it looked completely different. The staff at Unicorn were delighted and a lot of the patients also commented on how it was much more of a welcoming place than it had been in its previous guise.

TALL SHIPS

Aberdeen was lucky enough to see the Cutty Sark Tall Ships Race in 1991. The Cutty Sark Tall Ships Race aims to encourage international friendship and to train young people in the art of sailing. It is an annual event that is held in European waters and sees old ships sail or race over several hundred nautical miles. The race was the brainchild of a retired London solicitor, Bernard Morgan, who came up with the idea of bringing young cadets and seamen together from all around the globe to compete in an event that eventually became reality in 1956.

The race came to Aberdeen as a stop-off before it went on the final straight to Holland. The crew and their vessels stopped off in Aberdeen for three or four days. Thankfully, it wasn't like in the past where former seafarers would come off their boats, get drunk, get arrested and thrown in prison. So Craiginches didn't have to offer overnight accommodation this time around.

Aberdeen really got involved in the event and it brought thousands of visitors to the city. The prisoners also wanted to get involved. I am certain they wanted to be part of the feel-good factor rather than trying to stow away to warmer climes.

The famous Irish ship the *Asgard II* won the race that year, contributing most to the race and also by fostering international relations. We spoke to the prisoners and they wanted to present the *Asgard II* crew with something from their visit to Aberdeen. There was no point in giving them something decorative because the ship and their crew would be out on the high seas a lot. So they thought it would be better if they gave the crew something more practical. It was decided amongst the prisoners and staff that we would make them a present and then hand it over to their crew. We decided the best and most practical thing for the ship was bow fenders. For those, like myself, who aren't very nautical, bow fenders are giant protective bumpers, which are hung over the side of a ship to stop it berthing or crashing against the jetty or harbour where it is docked. We made seven bow fenders.

It was good because it allowed us to get some of the inmates involved. We selected two convicted prisoners who went down to make the presentation on the *Asgard II*. The whole prison felt part of that Tall Ships visit. Jim Robertson, our industries manager, made the presentation, which was fitting as he did a lot of sterling work throughout his years at the prison.

The *Asgard II* did manage one more visit to Aberdeen in the Cutty Sark Tall Ships race when it returned in 1997. I am sure the fenders would have been put to good use until the *Asgard* finally sank off the Bay of Biscay in 2008.

THE SALVATION ARMY BAND

We managed to persuade the Salvation Army to play a concert for an older lady called Annie Smith. An officer, Douglas Falconer, whose wife's mum had been in Kingseat Hospital was to be celebrating her eighty-third birthday there. So Douglas approached us and asked if there was anything we could do to help his mother-in-law to celebrate. He also said she was a big fan of the Salvation Army and their musical bands.

That made things slightly easier, as Leslie McBain and Norrie Page, who were both in the Salvation Army, worked with us at the prison. I went and asked them if this request would be possible and they said they would check it out at the Aberdeen Citadel, their city headquarters, and they came back and told us it wouldn't be a problem.

They got a large number of members from their band out and played a small concert for Annie and the rest of the patients on the hospital's Stuart Ward for more than an hour. She couldn't believe it. I think it's fair to say that was a birthday Annie and her family were never going to forget.

Her daughter, Moira Falconer, speaking at the time, said: 'She really enjoys singing hymns and we thought it would be really nice if she could hear some played. She loved it and you could see the other patients really appreciated it to. I am very grateful to the Salvation Army, the nursing staff and Craiginches Prison for putting in all the effort to make it happen.'

175

DICTAPHONES TO HELP THE LESS ABLE

The Craiginches Community Links was approached by dozens and dozens of different groups and charities looking for support. There were some big projects but there were also some smaller but just as important ones we assisted along the way.

We were able to go straight to the funds and to write out a cheque. One of those was when we donated money to a local group who helped support disabled young adults to buy four Dictaphone recording devices: the same recorders that journalists and newspaper reporters are seen using. That sort of donation didn't break the bank but even buying those four machines made a big difference to a lot of people.

This donation came about through a lady called Alison Tavendale. She actually worked on a voluntary basis in the prison with some of the inmates who maybe struggled mentally or physically with prison life. She did a really good job.

Alison also helped out with this group. If memory serves me correctly she was writer in residence.

The Dictaphones allowed the young adults to record their stories and work, which would then help the volunteers to put their poetry, literature or even their own biographies down on paper at a later date.

It was an important project because without such support it wouldn't have been possible for the young adults involved to carry out the work that obviously meant so much to them.

CONGO

There were often some smaller individual projects that some of the committee members would agree to take on themselves. Allan Grant was approached to help with the Grampian Seafood Fayre, which was held in Aberdeen. It was an event where companies and caterers came together to showcase the great food on offer in and around the waters of the North-east. It was a big thing and used to be held at the Aberdeen Exhibition and Conference Centre.

I am not sure if Allan was much of a fisherman but the organisers of the Grampian Seafood Fayre were looking to really spread the word ahead of their big launch. So they organised several high-profile events to raise awareness in and around the city.

They wanted to kick off the fayre with a giant parade through the centre of Aberdeen. That was where the approach to Alan came in. They asked if the prisoners could help make a giant eel which would provide the focal point of the 200-strong parade.

The prisoners were no strangers to showing off their creative talents by that point. They produced a giant eel's head that the organisers and volunteers were delighted with. It proved to be a real show-starter.

WE COULDN'T ALWAYS HELP

We used to get a lot of requests in to the committee. There were always conditions attached if we were to do a job. One or two of the committee would always go up and assess a job or an application. We wanted to help as many people as we could, which was why we set up the committee in the first place, but it was impossible to meet everyone's demands. The applications were just never ending. We always tried to pick the one that needed the most help. We felt that was the best and easiest way.

AWARD WINNERS

32

THE BUTLER TRUST

The Butler Trust is probably not that well known outside of the prison service but for those in that particular profession it is one of the highest accolades you can achieve.

The award was named after former home secretary Richard Austen Butler to celebrate outstanding dedication, skill and creativity by people working in correctional settings across the United Kingdom. Mr Butler was pivotal in a series of reforms in the late 1950s to improve the management, care and rehabilitation of offenders (as set out in his 1959 White Paper 'Penal Practice in a Changing Society') and understood the important role played by those who were in daily contact with such offenders.

Mr Butler went on to hold the role of deputy Prime Minister and after leaving office then wrote the 1975 Butler Report, which led to significant improvements in the management and care of offenders with a mental illness.

He was later rewarded for his work when he was named Lord Butler of Saffron Walden and was able to take his well-deserved seat in the House of Lords.

The Butler Trust was set up in his name in 1985 as a lasting tribute to the work he did in our particular sector. Her Royal

Highness Princess Anne agreed to become the patron from the very beginning. The three main people who helped to set up the trust were Veronica Linklater, who is now Baroness Linklater of Butterstone; Reverend Peter Timms OBE, who was a former prison governor; and David Astor, who was a former editor of the *Observer* newspaper.

The idea was to recognise and celebrate outstanding practice by those working with offenders through an annual award scheme. You were nominated for the award and then the committee considered each individual application.

I was put forward by the Craiginches governor at the time, Bill Rattray. He didn't tell me but I unofficially got a copy of his application letter. His opening was: 'I wish to nominate Bryan Glennie for the Butler Trust Award. I consider him to be an outstanding example of an officer who shows enthusiasm for his work and he is prepared to inconvenience himself so that others less fortunate may benefit.' He also went on to catalogue the reasons for my nomination. He listed my Control and Restraint Instructor training, how I had become a First Aid instructor, a Physical Training instructor, all the entertainment nights at Craiginches we had helped to organise and the outside projects with the prisoners. If I remember correctly he also included the prison visits and the boxing tournaments as part of my application.

I hadn't even been told my name had been put forward until I received a letter from the Butler Trust to invite me down to London for an interview as part of the process. Sir Trevor Brooking was one of the judging panel that particular year, along with the Archbishop of Canterbury, Robert Runcie, as chairman. There was also a lady there as well, apologies, I can't remember her name but she had been sold on the work we did at Burn O'Vat. She was impressed with the job we had done but I think she was also influenced by the fact she had a holiday home of her own nearby at Ballater. She had been to Burn O'Vat several times and she was able to vouch, first hand, of the work we had done.

My interview went well and I headed back to Scotland after it. I knew I had done all I could and sold the work we had done at HMP Aberdeen to the best of my ability. That proved to be the case, as I got word that I had been successful, which was a very humbling moment. I really couldn't believe it and it took a bit of time to sink in.

The letter read:

Dear Mr Glennie,

First of all, I am delighted to be able to add my congratulations to those of our Chairman (Sir Richard Butler) on your award.

Your award will be publicly presented to you in the form of a certificate by Her Royal Highness the Princess Royal at Lambeth Palace on Monday, March 12.

Now on to practical details. When replying to the invitation, could you please confirm your name and grade are correct at the head of this letter and also let us know the name of your companion, as we have to prepare a complete guest list for security purposes.

Can you please be at Lambeth Palace at 11.30 a.m. so that we can have a quick briefing and run through the procedure in the guard room?

As far as dress is concerned, if you normally wear uniform, this would be those who don't normally work in uniform, dark suits are probably best for the men and day dresses or suits for women. The Princess Royal has not worn a hat at previous award ceremonies but obviously this is a matter of individual taste.

After the presentation you and your guest will have the opportunity to meet the Princess informally and there will be a buffet lunch. It is a very happy occasion and I'm sure you will enjoy being such an important part of it. The Princess will leave about 2 p.m. and the rest of the guests shortly afterwards.

As an award winner, your travel expenses are borne by the Scottish Prison Department while the Butler Trust will pay your guest's expenses. Limited parking is also available within the Palace forecourt on request.

We very much look forward to hearing back from you and seeing you on the day.

Finally, we would also like to confirm that a copy of a letter of commendation from the Trust will be placed on your personal files.

Yours sincerely

Anna Humphrey

(Administrator with Butler Trust Award)

I went down to pick up my Butler Trust Award at Lambeth Palace, London, at noon on Monday 12th March 1990.

My wife and I arrived at the Guard Room, where we were introduced and given some last-minute reminders as to what to do and to expect. We were then taken through the main room, where we were given our programme of events and shown to our seats.

I opened up the programme and I couldn't quite believe what I was seeing. My name was the first one on the list. My name was there along with officers from all over the United Kingdom, from the Isle of Wight to Northern Ireland. It read:

Bryan Glennie, officer – HMP Aberdeen.

In addition to his work as a discipline officer, Mr Glennie has demonstrated unparalleled initiative and enthusiasm in every area of the life of the institution, constantly wishing to increase his own life skills and use them for the benefit of others. He is a first aid instructor, a qualified Physical Training instructor, one of five Scottish national Control and Restraint instructors, a gardens and education officer and has also been known to relieve catering staff. In his spare time, he has arranged a wide variety of entertainments with the establishment and also actively seeks out diverse projects for inmates within the community.

I have to say I was really, really humbled to see my name on the list – at all. Then to see everything on that list was actually quite embarrassing. I didn't do anything for self gain. Everything was done to try and help others or for the benefit of HM Prison Aberdeen or the Scottish Prison Service itself.

The chairman opened the ceremony and gave his introduction then he invited HRH Princess Royal forward to make her speech before she went on to present the awards. There was then a review of the Butler Trust Annual Report, a vote of thanks from trustee Sir Edward Ford before the ceremony was closed and we made our way to the Pink Drawing Room, where we met the Princess Royal and lunch was served.

After I got back to Aberdeen I also got a lovely letter from the Scottish Prison Officers' Association commending me on my Butler Award. It read:

Dear Bryan,

*The Executive Committee of the Scottish Prison Officers'
Association have asked me to extend on their behalf their*

warmest congratulations in regard to your recent achievement in the Butler Award Scheme.

It is awards such as this; to hard working, dedicated officers that the national press should be vigorously reporting rather than some of their more dubious stories.

Again, congratulations and all the best for the future.

Yours sincerely

Derek Turner
(Deputy General Secretary of the Scottish Prison Officers' Association)

33

THE ROYAL ROWIES

A rowie for those not acquainted with the north-east of Scotland is a savoury bread roll. It is also known as an Aberdeen roll, or in Aberdeenshire it is more commonly known as a buttery. Its main ingredients are flour, lard, butter or vegetable oil and yeast. It may not sound like the healthiest of eats but it has been a staple part of breakfasts in the North-east for well over a century.

It was first baked as an alternative to more traditional breads. The fishing community of the North-east was to be the main benefactor. They needed a bread or roll that had a longer shelf life and something that would last the rigours of two or three weeks at sea. The rowie proved to be the perfect solution as well as offering a tasty snack. Its high fat content also provided an immediate source of energy for some of our more hardened seafarers.

I knew the rowie was a favourite in the north-east of Scotland but I didn't know it was so famous further afield. In fact it, unofficially, has the royal seal of approval. I can vouch for that. I met Her Royal Highness Princess Anne, as you know, at the Butler Trust awards. She is a big supporter of our British prisons and has been its patron for more than thirty years. During that time, she has made more than 170 prison visits, including one to HMP Aberdeen, but we will go into that later.

I remember the morning of the presentation I had a real nervous excitement. Once I had got all the formalities out of the way – the royal protocol and greetings – I thought I was good to go. My name was called and, as instructed, I made my way up to the stage.

I was thinking, now Bryan, don't mess this up. I walked on to the stage and the Princess Royal then congratulated me on winning the award and presented me with my Butler Trust Award.

There was a buffet lunch after the ceremony and I met up with Princess Anne and had a chat with her. In the conversation it was mentioned that being from Aberdeen I would know about Aitken's rowies. I did tell her that Mrs Aitken was a big supporter of our work at HMP Aberdeen.

Princess Anne has been a big supporter of the British Prison Service and she knows her stuff. We got speaking and she asked me about our work at HMP Aberdeen. I told her about our work at Burn O'Vat. The Royals, of course, are no strangers to the North-east. They spend a lot of time at their royal residence of Balmoral Castle. I have to say, to her credit, she was more than aware of all the work we had done at Burn O'Vat. What intrigued her most of all was the work of the prisoners and how we were able to get them back out in the community. She asked if we had any problems on that front and I explained to her that the prisoners are told in advance that we have to have their trust and it works both ways.

When I went back into Aberdeen I popped in to see Mrs Aitken. We got on really well together and, as I said before, Aitken's Bakery had been a big help in supplying food for the different coffee mornings and fund-raisers we held at the prison. When I told Mrs Aitken the story she couldn't believe it. She told me that if I was ever going to meet Princess Anne again then to give her a shout and she would make sure I would have rowies for her.

Not too long after my Butler Trust Award I was invited down to a reception at Bute House in Edinburgh with Lord James Douglas-Hamilton, the Scottish minister. I had half an inclination that Princess Anne might be in attendance when I read the invitation. So I told this to Mrs Aitken and she said: 'No problem, I will get the rowies sorted out for you.' I went down to the shop and sure enough she gave me a big box of rowies that was decorated with ribbons and bows. I took them down to Edinburgh with me, guarding them with my life, making sure they were still in the same pristine condition as when Mrs Aitken had handed them to me.

When I went into Bute House, I was greeted by Lord James Douglas-Hamilton. I walked in with this big box and I had to tell him that, unfortunately, it wasn't a present for him. I explained that it was for Princess Anne and so one of her staff took it off me and put them in the kitchen for her.

When Princess Anne came in we all automatically stood up to be introduced to her and when it came to my turn I said: 'We meet again and I have remembered about Aitken's rowies. They are in the kitchen. But before that I want to talk to you about something else. I wondered if you could maybe assist HMP Aberdeen as we prepare to celebrate our centenary next year?' She then pointed me in the direction of one of her aides, who was next to Veronica Linklater of the Butler Trust awards. She came forward and we sat down and I explained we were going to celebrate Aberdeen Prison being one hundred the following year. We were organising a big event to celebrate it in a big way and wondered if the

Princess would be available to visit Craiginches to make it an even more special event. We had a long chat, I gave her all the details and she informed me that we would have to put in a formal letter of request with all the details and then they would get back to us.

I wasn't sure if that would be the last I would hear of Princess Anne paying a visit to HMP Aberdeen. How wrong I was – although our opening invitation was to end in disappointment.

I got all the details from Princess Anne's aide and I returned to Craiginches. I went in to see the governor, Bill Rattray, and explained there might be a chance we could end up getting a royal visit. Mr Rattray was equally thrilled and excited about that prospect and right away he sat down and started to type up a letter, as I had been instructed, to Lieutenant-Colonel Sir Peter Gibbs, the Princess Royal's secretary. Mr Rattray's letter on 29th July 1991 went like this:

I write on behalf of my prison officer Bryan Glennie, the chairman of the Aberdeen Prison Centenary Committee. Mr Glennie is a Butler Trust Award winner and at a recent reception for Scottish Award winners he approached Veronica Linklater of the Trust to ask if it would be possible for the Princess Royal to visit Aberdeen prison to mark the end of the prison's centenary year celebrations. Veronica suggested that Mr Glennie should write to yourself and, after discussions, he decided that I should make the approach on his behalf.

1991 is a very special year for us at Aberdeen Prison and we have just completed a very extensive programme of fund-raising for local charities. Additionally, prison staff located the original horse-drawn Black Maria which transported the first prisoners to Aberdeen prison. This was restored to its original state by staff and prisoners and was used as a focal point of a parade through the city on 9th June 1991.

Several other events were organised all of which were intended to raise money for charity whilst at the same time raising our community involvement profile. Consequently, Mr Glennie's suggestion would be a fitting tribute and end to the centenary year. What we had in mind was an informal visit where the Princess Royal could unveil a memorial board with the names of the governors of the establishment over the past 100 years.

I am aware that Royal visits, however, are not the simplest things to organise but feel confident that, having met the Princess Royal during a visit to HM Prison Shotts, she would be interested in what has happened in Aberdeen, particularly, as the chairman of the committee is also a Butler Trust Award winner. I have also spoken to Ruth Stone, the administrator for the Butler Trust. She advised me that the Princess Royal's visits to establishments under the auspices of the Butler Trust have been finalised and, therefore, it would not be possible to add Aberdeen at this time. She therefore suggested that we make the approach directly with yourself.

I look forward to your response,

W. A. R. Rattray
(Governor of HM Prison Aberdeen)

He didn't have to wait too long. In fact within a week I was summoned to the Governor's office, where he handed me the letter with the reply to read. It explained that her engagements were full up for the time of the centenary and with regret she was unable to attend. We did have plenty to organise for our centenary so it allowed more time for that.

It was a disappointment when we heard the news but we

always knew it was going to be something of a long shot, especially with all the time the Princess Royal dedicates to charities and good causes every year. We did think that would be the end of any hopes of a visit from the Princess Royal but how wrong we were!

34

THE CRAIGINCHES AWARD WINNERS

All our charitable work at Craiginches didn't go unnoticed either. We got a lot of local recognition. We were named as Scotland winner in the Business in the Community Awards. We were also specially commended for our work in their national awards for the public sector.

I don't actually know how we were nominated for any of the awards we received. We didn't apply ourselves and we can only surmise or speculate that it was the governor or somebody else at Craiginches. Nobody ever held up their hand and told us it was them. I still think it was the governor and my money would be on in him if I was a betting man, but I don't know 100 per cent.

It was great for the prison to get the recognition and awards we did. Allan Grant, one of the committee, was quoted in the *Evening Express* at the time. He said: 'It is good to see the staff and prisoners working together. When it comes to charity the prisoners are always eager to get involved.' We were invited down to the Business in the Community Awards presentation ceremony in London. It was to be held at the home of British Academy of Film and Television Awards (BAFTA). So Allan Grant, Ernie Christie and myself were more than happy to head to England's capital to pick up an award in recognition of the work done at Craiginches.

We flew down and stayed at my usual digs in Newbury Street, which was a short walk from the awards venue. It was a breakfast celebration so we were up and at it pretty early.

I speak on behalf of all three of us when I say we were honoured to go up and collect the top award: the British Employees in the Community Award. We also got a special commendation for our work at the ceremony, over and above the awards we picked up. It was a special occasion for all involved. The awards kept coming. Within a few weeks of getting back to Craiginches we got word that we had to go down to Grangemouth for a top Scottish award. We had been named as overall winners of the Scottish Business in the Community Awards. We were invited down to receive our award at a special reception which was held at the Grangemouth Oil Refinery near Falkirk.

So Allan MacKinnon and myself headed down the road. We were able to make full use of the accommodation at the Scottish Prison Service training college. We also had a special guest, Charlotte Leys from CLAN, who also did voluntary work at the prison, while governor Bill Rattray also came down on the day.

It was full of high flyers and it was great to know that HMP Aberdeen was going to take pride of place. It gave all four of us a tremendous boost and a real buzz, knowing all the hard work that had got Craiginches to this point. It had been a real team effort that had paid off with everything we had done and achieved. The awards were nice and the icing on the cake but they were pretty much secondary.

We had done a lot of good work but I remember our introduction ahead of our awards so vividly. The host explained how we had opened up the prison and brought the local community into events like the Burns Suppers and the Christmas Party.

A lot of emphasis was put on our work in the community, going out into the community, building bridges and also the high quality of work the prisoners had produced at Burn O'Vat and the building of the boardwalks at Bridge of Don.

It was a real team effort and every one of the Craiginches staff played their part some way along the line. We were just so lucky and fortunate during that period to have the staff we had. Nothing was impossible or too much trouble. We all just dug in and made things happen. Whether it was making things, dressing up or just volunteering their time. It was a joy to work for them. These awards were for every single one of our colleagues. The awards kept on coming. Sometime later Allan Grant from our committee was awarded an MBE not just for his work on our committee or the Black Maria but also for many years of dedication to the Scottish Prison Service – what a well deserved honour.

35

Representing Craiginches and Scotland

We also got major recognition for Craiginches on another front – our bowling. I actually first got involved in the sport not long after I had started work at the prison, having finally decided to up sticks and move the family to Aberdeen. We moved to a new three-bedroom house at Heathryfold West in the city. I had always thought about taking up bowling but my time was limited in Insch due to work, church, football and boxing commitments.

Now I was moving to the big city I thought it was as good a time as any to give it a try. The good thing with Aberdeen being a big city was that I was never going to be short of options. As you know, I became a member of the Aberdeen Royal Infirmary Bowling Club, which was the closest one to our new home, hence the reason we were able to get prisoners on to the green banks improvement project there a few years later. I have always loved bowling. It is a good sport. I have also been lucky enough to make some really great friends thanks to my time bowling.

My work at Aberdeen Royal Infirmary also took me down

another bowling route. Colin Mearns played out of Cults Bowling Club but he knew me very well. He asked me if I would like to do a course to become a bowling coach. I hadn't really given it much thought before. I had given people advice or a bit of guidance here or there but beyond that I had pretty much concentrated on my own game. I did have a think about his proposal and then I thought why not. I called him to tell him I had decided to take him up on his offer. A few weeks later it was all done and dusted and I had my coaching qualifications. I wanted to put them to full use so I started to coach new members at the ARI and I still continue to coach to this day. I do most of my coaching at my current club, Polmuir. I coach everyone from new members down to the coaching for the school children from the local school in Ferryhill. It would be good to see more and more people getting into the sport because it keeps you active, fit and competitive. I just love to see new people getting involved. It would be great if they could get as much out of bowling as I have throughout the years.

A lot of my bowling highlights come from bowling for the Scottish Prison Service's Bowling Association. It wasn't that long after I started at Craiginches that I got involved in the local and national competitions. We had a lot of good bowlers in the Aberdeen prison officers scene. They competed at various clubs in and around Aberdeen, which was good, especially when we went into the inter-prison tournaments, where we would play the staff from other similar establishments from across Scotland.

I bowled at Aberdeen Royal Infirmary with Gordon Tough, while Alex Baddenoch and Johnny Annand were out of Whitehall Bowling Club. That brought a bit of extra edge when it came to the individual competitions.

There would be pairs, fours and triples. The competitions

could be anywhere in Scotland from Stirling to Perth and beyond. We certainly clocked up the miles travelling from the North-east to play representatives from the prisons at Barlinnie, Peterhead, Inverness, Perth, Friarton and Edinburgh. All the Scottish competitions were really well attended.

The good thing was that the Aberdeen teams were always really competitive. I know because I was lucky enough to be part of teams who won the rinks and the triples three times. I played with Johnny and Alex in the triples. We gelled well as a team and we were always hard to beat.

I was also part of the side that won the Scottish Prison Service fours at the Tulloch Institute in Perth in 1990. Our successful team that year comprised Bill Watt, Bill Courage, Johnny Annand and myself. We played well throughout the competition to get our hands on the C. E. Health Cup. We beat Dumfries in the semi-final and got a big win over our local rivals, Peterhead, in the final. That particular trophy proved to be relatively lucky for Johnny and myself. We weren't able to defend our title but we did get our hands on it again a year later in 1992. So in those three years it spent a lot of time in the living rooms of Aberdeen. The second time around we beat Perth in the semi-final and then we got the better of Polmont in the final. So it is always a competition I look back on with a great fondness.

Another tournament I was lucky enough to win was the Scottish Prison Service Indoor Rinks Championship. I was in a team that included Bob Campbell senior, Sandy Scott and Scott Wheeler. The tournament was held down at the West Lothian Indoor Stadium in Livingston. It was funny because I didn't even know if I was going to have a team to play with in that particular competition. There was myself and Sandy Scott from Longriggend but apart from that we were still two short. We would have been all right for a pairs competition but we were sadly lacking for the fours. The problem was that two of our stalwarts, Gordon Tough and Johnny Annand, were playing at their own club competitions in Aberdeen that weekend and were unable to travel.

So it was a case of trying to find two new recruits who could come in. Most of the time it wasn't a problem, there was always someone who wanted to be involved, but with the shift system in prisons we were often short of players. I must say we were really lucky that day to manage to get a hold of the two players we did.

We managed to get a team made up with Bob Campbell senior, who played his bowls at Perth, and Scott Wheeler, who played at Newhills in Aberdeen.Experienced bowlers know that it is a far different game going from indoor to outdoor or vice versa.

I couldn't believe it. None of us expected to gel and play quite as well as we did. I certainly never had any thoughts about winning when I went into the competition. I was just relieved we had a team and I was getting a game. We started strongly and the confidence just grew and that took us all the way.

We did really well and managed to beat Stuart Little's Glenochil team 4–3 in the final to lift the James Strang Trophy. We came out top of twenty-three other teams – not bad for a team that was only put together at the last minute.

Sandy Scott was another extended member of the Aberdeen bowling team. There were only a handful of players in Sandy's area and so he was always delighted to take our call. The good thing was that he was an exceptional bowler and so we knew when he came in he would just strengthen our team.

A lot of our staff did get a bit tired of the travelling down to the Central Belt and further afield when there were so many competitions in the Central Belt, so it was good to have others to call on because the prison bowling was another big commitment.

The bowlers were also selected to play our annual games against the Scottish Police Service. They were also competitive affairs, with both teams desperate for the upper hand.

The inter-prison tournaments, though, continued to be the main events in the Craiginches' bowling calendar. Success in those domestic competitions also opened other doors and lifted things to a whole new level.

There was the annual international tie against the English Prison Service. One year it would be in Scotland and the next it was England and so on. We thought it was the fairest way and allowed people to come and visit and see parts of the country they wouldn't normally. It was also a good way to strengthen relations between the Scottish and English prison services.

It wasn't, however, just a straight selection policy. It was far more regimented than that. You had to earn your place and the only real way to guarantee your spot was to make an impression in the national tournaments.

It was done on a points basis. You would be given ranking points if you got so far in a tournament. You would get more points the further you went and even more if you won it. The top points winners at the end of each season were then guaranteed their place in the team. So you knew if you played well and consistently throughout the year you would be fine, but if you didn't it was a long and anxious wait.

The selectors would then have a few wild card selections like the captains have in golf's Ryder Cup. They then hand-picked players from other prisons to make up the rest of the team.

The Scottish Prison Bowling Association was organised by

a committee and led by Bob Campbell, who was originally from Perth. The job Bob and his team did in organising all these events and games was fantastic. They sorted your accommodation and your transport and everything else in between. They really were an excellent committee and their organising skills were first class. The Scottish team was also well turned out and we had a few sponsors. One year Slater's menswear kitted us out and this year, 2017, they celebrate twenty-five years since it was formed.

We seemed to be dressed for success out on the rink against the Auld Enemy as well.

In my time against England we only lost two internationals and I think I played about seventeen times against them. If I remember correctly the first fixture was in 1992, when we won at Alnwick. From then on it became an annual event.

I played that first year with Derek Stewart in my rinks team. Derek was also from Aberdeen and he played out of Portlethen Bowling Club. We did well together but so did most of our teams.

It did irk the England teams when they lost but the good thing was it was an annual competition so they got their chance for revenge the next year. They never had that long to wait. Also, once we left the rink it was all forgotten and we would have a social event all together and a few light refreshments.

The following year the return was on home soil with Bridge of Allan chosen as the venue where we were looking to defend our crown. The committee continued to work tirelessly and managed to bring in Black Bottle Whisky as the international match sponsor. I certainly appeared confident that we would win. The local press did an article on the game. I was quoted in the *Evening Express* as having said: 'Having hammered England on their own territory, we will be looking for a double.' We did win in Bridge of Allan but it wasn't all success and when we lost to England it was a big thing. I recall the first time they beat us. We had won the first two meetings and we were looking to make it a glorious hat-trick but we fell just short of the mark.

The match that year was in Leicester, at the Knighton Victoria Bowling Club, so it meant that much more to the England team not to lose at home again. It was harder for us to take, as it was a tight affair, and in the end five shots were the only difference between the teams.

We usually delayed coming back up the road from England because we played a friendly on the Sunday and would return to Scotland on the Monday. That year we played Warwickshire County Vice-presidents Association at Bilton Bowling Club. That was a bit flatter than normal after we had lost the big one in the Midlands.

The next year we were back up in Scotland. Bridge of Allan was the venue and we hoped it would bring us continued luck. I remember the *Evening Express* and the *Press and Journal* newspapers, which in fairness gave our prison bowling great coverage, made a big thing about that follow-up match. It helped that there were quite a few Aberdeen players in the team.

Jim Stephen, Alec Badenoch and myself were all selected for international duty at Bridge of Allan.

I remember I was quoted in the *Evening Express* at great length. I was certainly fired up for the game. I said: 'It is always a great honour to be selected for Scotland, and this match – which we like to refer to as a "serious friendly" – means a great deal to us. Our defeat by just five shots last year was really hard to swallow, particularly as we were going for a hat-trick of wins. So everyone is really keyed up and out to get revenge on home territory. It's bound to be a tough match as England have a very strong association – we only have twenty-one jails to choose from, while they have 121. But we have to go into the game confident. The team played a practice match at Bridge of Allan recently and although we lost, it was a very useful exercise.'

Thankfully we managed to get the trophy back and ensured it remained in Scotland for another twelve months, and I wasn't left with egg on my face. We won 124 shots to ninety-five to make it a pretty comprehensive victory.

I was quoted again by the *Evening Express*. I added: 'Defeat last year was a bitter pill to swallow and we certainly didn't want to lose at home this time. That spurred us on. A few of the English team said they were overwhelmed by the enthusiasm of our team.'

All of the team got decent local press exposure. It was also added to, at that time, by the *Green Final*, which was the local Saturday evening results newspaper. That is now very much a thing of the past in Scotland, with everything pretty much at your fingertips thanks to television, radio, computers, tablets and the internet. You can now see the goals and games as they happen but back then you struggled to get match reports.

The *Green Final* was also good to give extra spots to your maybe lesser sports. It was certainly a welcome outlet for the Aberdeen bowling scene. They did a good article with Johnny Annand back in 1997 as he prepared to make his debut for the Scottish Prison Service. That year we were to travel south of the border with Rugby the chosen venue by our English hosts. The newspaper article came complete with a photograph of the team: John, Alex Badenoch, Gordon Tough, who was making his international debut, and myself.

John was quoted widely. He said: 'You always look to do your best against any team, but facing England adds that extra little something. Every Scot wants to put one over on the Sassenachs. Having spoken to some of the team in competitions this year, they feel we can go down there and do it because we are better organised than ever. To beat them on their own patch really would be something because they are sure to be that wee bit stronger.'

That proved to be another successful away day for the Scottish Prison team. We won in Rugby by forty-eight shots to take a 4–1 lead over our English counterparts. I also got in on the act. I spoke to the *Evening Express* in the wake of our win. I confirmed: 'The team spirit on the bus on the way down to Rugby was just amazing and I just couldn't see us losing it. We really went in with a very professional attitude this time around. There were a number of lessons learned from our last trip to England. We had a team meeting in the morning and did a wee huddle in the middle of the green. Everyone knew what we had to do. And any socialising before the game had been kept to a minimum.'

Another victory at Rugby was even more special. I was presented with a special plaque as one of only four players to have played for the Scottish Prison Service ten times. It was another great honour and was something of a surprise when my teammates got round me to make the presentation. I honestly didn't realise I had played that many times for Scotland and it really was a surprise albeit a rather pleasant one – especially after our win.

I continued to play for Scotland and in the bowling competitions after I had retired from the Scottish Prison Service, which was a good way for me to keep in touch with a lot of my former colleagues.

CENTENARY
CELEBRATIONS

36

THE CENTENARY

We had all our plans in place to make 1991 a year to remember and to make it a centenary celebration worthy of marking 100 years of Her Majesty's Prison Aberdeen. The prison had its own mission statement, and the centenary committee had one of its own aswell, both running parallel to each other.

The mission statement of HMP Aberdeen was:

We inspire to an environment in which dignity, respect and humanity all prevail; developing a range of options which allows each individual to achieve their full potential within an atmosphere that fosters good inter-personal relationships and a spirit of shared enterprise; within a framework of humane containment we aim to create for both staff and inmates alike an organisation with a management style which is open and accountable, just and safe for all.

The centenary year committee's mission statement was :

The aim of the Centenary Year Committee is to provide a series of events which will provide fun, entertainment and fund-raising in the build-up to 9th June, 1991, when we will commemorate the initial transportation of male and female convicts dressed in a typical garb of that period across the city of Aberdeen from the Old East Prison to Craiginches in Torry, turning the old 1891 flitting into 1991 entertainment.

The ultimate aim is for a 'Good time to be had by all.'

The centenary committee held several meetings. We had started to look at how we could mark the occasion. We put several things in place but we quickly realised with the way things were taking off the committee was never going to be able to cope with everything on its own.

We knew we needed more help so we asked for officers to become involved with the committee. That would be the only way we would be able to realise our dream because it was going to be such a massive project. We also had a prisoner on the committee because we thought it was important to give the prisoners an input.

We had several meetings and discussions as to the things we could do to mark the centenary. One of the original and main ideas was to try and locate the original Black Maria, a horse-drawn prison cart, and to try and restore it to its prime. We knew that was a long shot and if we couldn't get the original one then we wanted to get one of the same period that we could use because we knew it could be central to the festivities. That turned into a story in itself that I will go into in greater detail later on and that project was taken on by Allan Grant, assisted by Ernie Christie.

It was agreed that 9th June 1991 would be at the heart of the celebrations, as it was 100 years to the day since Craiginches had been put into service. It was a day in Craiginches' history that we couldn't let pass without marking it as a special event.

So we agreed that we would re-enact that first journey of the Black Maria from the city jail to Craiginches. The idea was to get people dressed up in period costume and to make it a day to remember.

We also wanted to return the prison bell that was removed after the rooftop protest, and our other thought was to get a centenary plaque to mark the prison's first 100 years.

Everything took a lot of hard work and planning.

We kicked off the centenary party at the Castlegate, at the top end of Union Street in Aberdeen city centre. We had traditional prison stocks and a number of entertainers on duty. The Buchan Heritage Society performed some bothy ballads then a local folk band, Broke-In-Spoke, did some numbers. There were also fine performances from the Bon Accord Cloggies dance group and a firefighting display from Grampian Fire Brigade. So we had a diverse range of entertainment for everyone.

We also got a lot of the local schools involved to do a number of poetry readings. That kept things ticking over to the main event – the re-enactment of the maiden journey to Craiginches. Our officers, Allan Grant and Bill Stephen, were decked out in old Victorian prison uniforms and led the procession. The Black Maria was led by an Irish cob horse called June which we had borrowed from the Duthie Park.

The only thing we were lacking was a prisoner. So we locked the local television personality and radio disc jockey, Robin Galloway, up in the Black Maria, along with local entertainer, Jim Rosie, and took them from the Castlegate back to the prison.

Robin was on Northsound One at the time. He took a keen interest in our work and how things were progressing. He gave us a lot of publicity and that was why we asked if he would be our prisoner for the day in our centenary event. The Black Maria headed a cavalcade of vintage vehicles that followed in the parade back to the prison.

Speaking to the *Press and Journal*, I said: 'It was a beautiful climax to a lot of hard work which was put in by a lot of people.'We held a sports day that ended with a barbecue for the prisoners. The prisoners did various runs, activities and sporting events. They loved it because it was a break from the normal mundane prison routine. The prison staff, headed by Norrie Page and his other kitchen staff, did the barbecue, which again gave them something different from the more traditional prison food.

We also wanted a permanent reminder of the centenary stone in the front wall of the prison beside the entrance. So Alex Gray, the works boss, got a special stone engraved. On our arrival back from the parade the Scottish Prison Service deputy director Alan Walker unveiled a Granite stone commemorating the prison's 100th birthday.

Alan made a major statement with his speech ahead of the unveiling. He said: 'Aberdeen prison is the "jewel in the crown of the Scottish Prison Service."' I have to say it was a humbling statement for all the staff and committee members who had worked so hard and put so much effort into making Craiginches the success it was.

Alan also wrote a letter to the governor Leslie McBain to thank him for the hospitality that had been shown to him and his wife during his visit.

He wrote:

I should like to express my appreciation to you and your staff for the friendly and courteous manner in which you looked after my wife and I at your recent centenary celebrations. Perhaps you would allow me, through the medium of your Governors Order Book, to express my commendation to all members of staff, especially Mr Glennie.

Every element appeared to work so well from the routine

administration to the unveiling ceremony and I am aware these matters were the result of extremely careful and thorough planning and are not left to chance.

On our way home we experienced torrential rain the like of which I have not seen since my days in Africa. I was a little puzzled why it held off during the ceremony. It did cross my mind that perhaps the Salvation Army and members of Aberdeen Prison had negotiated the timing of the rain with a 'higher place'.

Thank you again

Alan Walker

As part of our centenary year we also opened a shop unit in Aberdeen's Trinity Shopping Centre.

It allowed us to display some of the memorabilia that we had collected or had been donated to Craiginches through the years.

There was an empty unit within the Trinity Centre so we just approached their management and explained why we wanted the shop and asked if we could have it. Thankfully, they agreed and we got it rent-free.

We had to fall back on Alex Gray again because it was just a shell, left over from the previous occupants of the shop. Alex got involved and got some of his tradesmen up to our unit in the centre. They kitted it out, allowing us to have our exhibition. Alex was such a valuable member of our team and the contribution his tradesmen made to our cause was fantastic. We had hundreds and hundreds of people visit the display and they were amazed at what went on in the prison. They, like most others, thought Craiginches held prisoners and that was it.

We put out all our prison memorabilia and photographs to give people a real flavour of things at Craiginches. We were also assisted by the Scottish Prison Service Training College, who had a tremendous collection in its own archives. Peterhead Prison also helped. They gave us a matchstick model of St Machar's Cathedral in Aberdeen. It was solely made out of matchsticks by a prisoner. It was quite a common pastime amongst inmates. It was also a real skill.

Bill Fearnley, who was a deputy director for training and organisational development support for the Scottish Prison Service, also paid Craiginches a visit in our centenary. He seemed to be impressed with our shop unit. He later sent a letter to our governor, Leslie McBain. It read:

After all the earlier trials and tribulations, my reception yesterday by you and your colleagues and the valuable insights I got into what makes training tick at Aberdeen (and other things which might help to make the tick louder) meant a very enjoyable and wholly worthwhile visit. Thank you and please convey my gratitude to everyone concerned.

John Watt (to whom I have also written) has probably told you that we went to the centenary exhibition to round off my visit. I thought the exhibition had everything – visual appeal, excellent exhibits, a telling message and two worthwhile causes to support. I have to congratulate Bryan Glennie and his organising committee on their superb production.

Yours sincerely
Bill Fearnley

The other thing we wanted to do was to get the prison bell back up. The big brass bell had been out of commission for near enough twenty years after our infamous rooftop protest of 1972. It had been kept in storage since it was removed. It was all polished, cleaned and gleaming when it was put back up with all its original fittings at the entrance to A Hall.

The other major event we had organised was a centenary dinner dance. We held the event at the Douglas Hotel in Market Street. More than 200 staff, ex-colleagues and others from Peterhead and further afield attended. It was another great night and was more of a reward for the staff and those involved with the prison.

37

BLACK MARIA

O, Black Maria, I love you;
Mony's the time ye've hurlt me when I've been fu.
Seven an' seven's fourteen, an' seven's twenty one.
An' I've been aff ti Craigie-aigie-inches in the four-wheeled van.

A letter was published in the *Press and Journal* newspaper
from an elderly gentleman called Ian Bremner from Leslie,
Fife, who remembered this song being sung as a child by a
travelling entertainer in his local village hall.

When we got the committee together for our centenary, we
wanted something with links to Craiginches from the very
early years.

It was very much a celebration of then and now and we
wanted to portray that. So we had to think long and hard
as to what we could incorporate into our plans to give the
general reflection of the prison through the years.

Allan Grant, who was on the committee, was doing a bit
about the history of the prison for our landmark project. He
quickly found the Black Maria was very prominent in the
history of Craiginches. It was a horse-drawn prison cart that

used to transport the prisoners from the city court to the jail or between jails. It was used by the prison service and also by the police. The Black Maria was first introduced into the United Kingdom in the 1820s. It was first used at Craiginches around 1891 to take the prisoners on the roughly two-mile trip from the court to the prison.

The main body of the Black Maria was made of wood and was fitted to carry six prisoners in small individual cells. It had no windows, with a small roof ventilator offering limited air.

The Black Maria's name goes back to America in the 1840s. It centres round Maria Lee, who was the black owner of a lodging house in Boston, Massachusetts.

The story goes that she was always on to the police and authorities, letting them know when one of her residents or somebody in the community was up to no good. She was basically an informant.

The police horse and two-wheeled cart was always at her door so that it got the nickname Black Maria, both in the United States of America and in the United Kingdom.

Allan took a keen interest in our own Black Maria. He knew the prison used to have one and tried to find out what had happened to it. Allan worked closely with the Grampian Police historian and made real inroads to the whereabouts of our own original Black Maria.

Amazingly, he managed to discover its actual whereabouts. That in itself was a major feat because most of us thought the Black Maria would have long since been scrapped. It was discovered out in Peterculter, thanks to some homework the police historian had done.

There was a fair bit of excitement about his discovery but that quickly disappeared when we went out to have a look at the Black Maria. It is fair to say it wasn't in the best of conditions. It was an absolute wreck and any restoration dreams looked a near impossibility. All the wooden panels were wrecked, with broken roof felt everywhere and damp throughout.

It was no wonder the Black Maria was out in a farmer's yard and was being used as a makeshift henhouse. The Black Maria as I have explained had history but this particular one had had a less conventional one in recent years.

After it had been put out of commission it was used as a garden shed and even had a sink fitted inside it. Then it was moved out to Peterculter during the Second World War.

It had been initially used as a farmyard store but by the time we had got there it had been relegated to a chicken coup. In fairness, I don't even know if it was fit for that!

We then went and spoke to the local farmer who owned the Black Maria. We had a prisoner on the committee and we actually took him out with us to see the Black Maria. His comments and reaction when he first saw it pretty much sums up the state it was in. He had us all just about doubled up with laughter when he said: 'What the hell is this? What are we meant to do with this?' The members of the committee explained they were looking to get the Black Maria back but the farmer was having none of it. He just said he didn't want to sell it. It wasn't as if it was a family heirloom that was going to make him thousands of pounds in the future. We were actually doing him and his chickens a favour!

Ernie Christie, another of the committee, and Allan Grant finally persuaded the farmer to hand it over, although it cost us £10 for the pleasure. I would love to say it was a bargain. It wasn't back then but looking back now it has proved to be something of a real snip.

So with the transaction completed, we went out to Peterculter with Ernie's trailer and took the Black Maria back home. When we got back to Craiginches and saw the extent of the work we had to do we were left wondering if it was really going to be worth it. Was there any chance of restoring this battered old cart to its former glory? Remember this was about a year before the centenary celebrations and we didn't have long to deliver.

We didn't really know where to start. We were just thankful George MacAllan, the work shed boss at the prison, managed to empty an out-shed for us to store the Black Maria. Alex Gray, the works boss, was a huge help. He even gave us the use of his tradesmen and they all worked on it for weeks and weeks and started to get it repaired. Allan Grant had also continued his own research and he found a craftsman at Stonehaven who made two brand new wheel hubs for us, including all the individual wooden spokes, before he got somebody else from Pitcaple in Aberdeenshire to donate a metal wheel axle. We also got a blacksmith from Kirkton of Skene to finish the wheels off by putting the metal rims round them. Things were suddenly beginning to take shape and the impossible was looking possible.

Once we got the bodywork all done and the wheels sorted they took it down to a company called Gemini in Stonehaven to get it painted its trademark black. They also managed to get the royal emblems painted on the side panels. It was a major operation and took months.

We were lucky we had so many skilled tradesmen at our disposal in the prison. Allan also made sure he had everything in hand when it came to sourcing the more troublesome parts. We were also able to dip into the prison's common goods fund. It was money that was available to help good causes or things which would help raise the profile of the prison. The governor, Leslie McBain, took care of that for us.

Allan in particular took the Black Maria as his own project

and he gave it his all. Everyone can now see the end product and it is fair to say he and everyone connected with the restoration did themselves and the prison proud.

The Black Maria was central to our celebrations and actually became a bit of a minor celebrity in its own right. It even appeared in the BBC drama *Micawber*, which starred David Jason and was filmed in Edinburgh.

After the centenary celebrations were done and dusted, we wondered what we would do with the Black Maria. It was initially put on display at various sites across the North-east, including the Transport Museum out at Alford.

The Prison Museum at Inverary had earlier posted an interest in the Black Maria and requested it be put there. It was refused at that point as there were events at Irvine in Ayrshire and Fraserburgh Festival for horse-drawn vintage vehicles that it had been booked to attend that year.

After that it was kept in storage at our sister prison, HMP Peterhead, because we had nowhere to keep it at Craiginches. It remained in the Blue Toon until it was announced that both remaining prisons were to close.

The decision about what to do with the restored Black Maria was left to Archie Orr, a Principal Officer at Craiginches. The two remaining lads on the committee, Ernie Christie and Allan Mackinnon, had moved on to the open prison at Noranside, and Allan Grant, who had restored it, and I had both retired from the service. After all the work that went in to restoring it, it was a big decision. We wanted to make sure it was looked after and shown off in all its glory, not left to go to wrack and ruin like had happened when it was initially put out of commission all those years ago. Ernie and Allan left instructions with Archie to contact Inverary to see if they were still interested and, if so, they could arrange to have it picked up and taken down. They also knew if the Black Maria was left in the prison when the demolishing teams came in it would end up with the same fate as the old prisons themselves. We had done a lot of work and they wanted people to continue to see it in its full glory. They didn't want to see it falling into disrepair as had happened in the first instance.

It was no surprise that Inverary Prison agreed to take the Black Maria because they knew it would be a real Jewel in their Crown.

It may sound a match made in heaven but there was one small headache. How were they going to get the Black Maria into Inverary? That was a minor operation in itself. The vintage cart was lifted over the 12-foot prison walls by a hired crane because there were no double doors or entrances big enough to roll it directly in. It is now situated in the courtyard of the prison.

38

CENTENARY BENEFICIARIES

The centenary was a celebration, but we also saw it as a key vehicle through which we could help others. From the centenary book for Her Majesty's Prison Aberdeen:

> *We specialists in the care of offenders are going all out to raise money in support of Aberdeen's indispensable Childhood Leukaemia Unit because we believe that if, through our efforts, treatment can be improved for just one child, then our fundraising will be worthwhile.*
>
> *Based in Ward 4 of Aberdeen Sick Children's Hospital, it administers treatment to children from Grampian, Orkney, Shetland, and Highland regions. This valuable facility not only specialises in the care of children, it also cares for the family relationships of the young Leukaemia victims and uses its awareness of all the implications which that fatal disease will have for the family unit to strengthen the fortitude of its members.*

The fight against leukaemia was always one that pulled on the heartstrings at HMP Aberdeen. When it came to our centenary fund-raising it quickly came to the fore again. This time we decided to try and raise money for child sufferers. So we got in touch with Aberdeen Royal Infirmary again and they put us in touch with Ward 4.

They explained how it would make a big difference to their patients if they were able to bring in a couple of PC2 dual volumetric pumps. They were pumps which allowed nurses and the patients to set the precise dosage of any drugs that were being administered. We raised £3,000 and then a further £1,500.

As well as the equipment, we also raised money for Ward 4, which was one of the children's wards at Aberdeen Royal Infirmary. We had close links with Ward 4. They came through an officer whose wife worked with sick kids. It all kicked off when she asked if we could come along and entertain the ward one afternoon.

Bill Duncan, who did the disco at our centenary dance, also did a bit of amateur magician work on the side. I got him on board and we would go up and take sweets and balloons and play games and entertain the children for an hour or two at a time over the space of a good few months.

I used to come out and sit in the car and put my head in my hands and a few tears used to fall after we had been with them and it's something I am not ashamed to tell you. I was so touched by them. Some of the children were battling for their lives with illnesses like leukaemia and cancer but the welcome and spirit they gave you when you were there was just unbelievable. They had something special about them. They continued with life as if there was nothing wrong with them.

It was heartbreaking because you would find out that this boy or girl had passed away since your last visit.

It was from there we started to raise more funds for Ward

4. It touched the prison staff and it was clear that this was another project for which we didn't have any problems raising money. We raised money initially for drips.

A lot of the money from the centenary celebrations went to Ward 4. We had all the usual fund-raisers and also one with a difference. You were able to pour a bucket of porridge over an officer's head in the Trinity Centre for a £1 donation. All the money from there went to Ward 4.

39

The Royal Seal of Approval

We were all delighted with the way HMP Aberdeen's centenary had been marked. It was celebrated in some style, there had been no doubt about that. A lot of hard work and planning had gone into making it the undoubted success it had been. We were happy with what we had done and didn't think there was much more we could have done to cap things off until we got an unexpected and a more than welcome surprise dropping through the letter box at Craiginches.

Her Royal Highness Princess Royal wasn't for letting the prison, or myself, down after all. An official letter with the royal seal was delivered and confirmed Princess Anne had booked in several official engagements in Aberdeen. We were all thrilled to learn that a visit to Craiginches was one of them. She was to visit a fish processing plant first, then the prison and she was to sign off her day in the North-east by attending a centenary service at St Mark's Church. The joke from the minister at St Mark's, Reverend John Watson, that day was that the three places Princess Anne had visited were known locally as 'education, salvation and damnation'.

We had always hoped we would get Princess Anne. We couldn't quite believe it when the governor, Bill Rattray, told us of her intended visit. I was still in a bit of shock but at the same time I was absolutely delighted because I knew how massive a thing it was and it would be an unforgettable day in the history of the prison.

The news certainly helped to lift the obvious lull around Craiginches after all the excitement of the centenary had started to fade away. It was a great boost but it also meant more work for us, not that we were complaining, as the Centenary Links Committee went back to the drawing board to see if we could put a plan of action in place for our special guest.

We were still active with our fund-raising efforts but we wanted to make it a day to remember for the Princess Royal and to make sure Craiginches lived up to all the hype. I had told her all about the things we had done and were doing in our previous meetings and conversations together at the Butler Trust Awards and then at Bute House.

When you speak to Princess Anne she is a lovely, caring person and very accommodating. I was disappointed when we couldn't get her up for our centenary but when I look back things probably worked out even better with the visit coming after the centenary. We had more than enough to attend to with the celebrations. The good thing was that the following year the prison was back to near normality and we were able to put more time and organisation into our royal visit.

We had to get our side of things sorted out and worked in tandem with the police and the royals' security chiefs. They had planned everything for Princess Anne and, in all honesty, it was just like a normal day at the prison, outside of the things we had organised for the visit, which we were told would probably be no more than a couple of hours.

We sat down as a committee and with governor to try and think of the best things we could do to show her the good work that we had done and were doing in and around Craiginches. The governor, Bill Rattray, was going to take her for a walk round the workshops of the prison and then after that we would show her the Black Maria and she would sign off by unveiling a special plaque to commemorate her visit. Whistle-stop would be a fair description as we had so many things to fit in.

We did all our pre-planning and made sure everything was ready for Princess Anne. We decided to make full use of the photographs and things from our slide show that we took out into the community. We also had photographs up from the Butler Trust Award ceremony but believe me that was the governor's doing. They had nothing to do with me. The visit was confirmed for 20th March 1992.

So when the Princess Royal came into the prison she was welcomed by the governor and he then led her into the prison chapel to begin her tour. We had set out the visual displays in the chapel with a sample of some of the arts and crafts that were produced within the workshops of the prison, including football and army camouflage and items from the knitting shop, which showed her the quality of the work done in prison.

We then put some further photographs, pictures and displays up around the chapel. They showed all the work the prisoners had done up at Burn O'Vat and Balmedie Beach in our outside projects.

I had quite a chat with Princess Anne, as we shared some time in the chapel. She was especially impressed with the outside projects we had managed to get the prisoners involved in. Seeing all the photographs of the prisoners at work and then the finished projects made it that bit more real. It allowed her to get more of a flavour of things. She insisted the work we had done had been fantastic and she admitted it would be great if more prisons adopted similar projects and engagements with their outside communities.

We then took the Princess on a tour around the prison, including the workshops. Some of the prisoners, as you may recall, made bow fenders for the *Asgard II* when it came to Aberdeen for the Cutty Sark Tall Ships Race. We were also aware the Princess Royal had recently purchased a new boat of her own, named the *Blue Doublet*. It was named Doublet as that was the horse on which she won the European Eventing Championships back in 1971.

George MacAllan, the boss of the main work shed, decided it would be a good idea to make special bow fenders for the latest addition to the royal fleet. They made a great job of them but we'd come to expect nothing less from them. He then put the bow fenders proudly on display in the chapel. He left them hanging up so the Princess Royal could see them when she walked round the room. She looked around and then set her gaze on the bow fenders. George waited a couple of minutes then asked her: 'Do you like them?' She replied in the affirmative and he said: 'I am relieved about that because we made them for you, as a thank you for visiting the prison.' Princess Anne was delighted. That brought a massive smile to her face and George turned to one of her following aides and said: 'You better make sure there is plenty of room in the boot of the car for these.'

The kitchen staff then provided everybody with tea and coffee and Princess Anne cut a cake which had been specially baked for the event.

Princess Anne was then told about some of the other work we carried out before she was taken out to the courtyard to see our pride and joy – the Black Maria. The Black Maria was out again in its full glory. We had it all polished and cleaned and again had got a loan of a horse from the Duthie Park. We harnessed the horse up to the Black Maria inside the inner gate of the prison. We also got some of the male and female staff, Ernie Christie and Tracy Riddoch, dressed up in the period uniforms we had used for the centenary.

We put photographs on display inside the Black Maria from when it had been used as a hen house and then through the various stages of its restoration. It just showed her the work we had painstakingly put in. She had a good look around it and she had her picture taken with it too. She took a great interest and really couldn't believe the transformation in the Black Maria. Not many people could.

She then unveiled a plaque inside the gate reception area of the prison which stated the date of her visit and also a board that listed all the previous governors at Craiginches. They were both nice and lasting tributes. One of the female office staff, Kim Garland, then presented Princess Anne with a bouquet and she had her official press photographs taken. Her final engagement was to sign our visitors' book. There were a few more snaps of that taken and then she said her thank yous and farewells and was on her way, with her flowers, bow fenders and more importantly her Aitken's rowies. I had nipped round to get a special box of rowies made up from Mrs Aitken. I was not going to let Princess Anne go home without them. It just made sure it was the perfect day for her and everybody else at HMP Aberdeen.

I think the day was summed up when my colleague and my fellow bowler, Gordon Tough, retired. Huntly-born Gordon worked as a senior catering officer at Craiginches for more than thirty years. The *Press and Journal* newspaper did a piece on Gordon as he hung up his cooking apron and chef's hat for good.

He said: 'My highlight, just before I retired, was being introduced to Princess Anne when she visited the prison.

That, for me, says everything and what Princess Anne's visit meant to everyone at Craiginches.'

It was the same when we lost the ever resourceful Alex Gray from our ranks. He had been a massive influence at the prison and a major driving force on the centenary committee. We would never have managed without his help. Alex decided to take on a promotion and moved down to the Central Belt to take charge of the Polmont Young Offender's Institute Works Department.

We knew we had to give Alex a send-off to remember. So we got the Black Maria, which he had helped us to restore, and took photographs of Alex sitting on it. We also presented Alex with a framed photograph of Princess Anne being shown round the Black Maria that day. So it is fair to say her visit lives long in the lives of most of the staff.

THE END

40

My Retirement

I was working down at the Scottish Prison Service College at Polmont, near Falkirk, on another secondment. That was back in 1995. One of the tutors had broken his ankle and I was asked to fill in by my old friend George Laird. I enjoyed going down to the training college because it was a lot different from my daily work at Craiginches. I went down as cover and ended up down there for even longer than I had thought! While the officer had been off recovering from his accident he had ended up landing another post as an assistant governor at Craiginches. I am not sure if he was classing that as a lucky break or not! But it could have been a lot worse.

When I was down covering we had a departmental visit from the head office. I remember it was quite a big thing and all the tutors were lined up to be introduced. There was also a member of staff from the Scottish Prison Service's personnel department. This gentleman, I can't remember his name but he was high up in the personnel department of the Scottish Prison Service, shook my hand and asked about my service, where I had been and worked. We got speaking and I gave him a brief history of my career in the prison service. I then told him how I had worked with the

Post Office before that and how I had managed to transfer my service from there.

He listened to me and then said: 'So why are you still with the SPS? You have been here a long time.' He then said: 'I am sure you would be able to retire if you wanted to.' Before he left he signed off by saying: 'Leave this with me.'

He was true to his word. He looked into my circumstances and then came back to me. He said: 'You are at the maximum for your pension and all your benefits. You can stay on and work until you are fifty-five but it wouldn't make any difference to your pension or anything else.' He said: 'If I was you I would retire.' Maybe that was his way of politely saying go before you are pushed but I think he was genuinely looking out for me.

By that time I had just turned fifty-three and in terms of the prison service I was very much in the twilight years of my career. I took time and discussed things with the family and then had a long hard think about things. I then made my decision that I was going to retire. It was a no brainer, if I am being honest. It wasn't a hard decision in the end. I could have stayed on for another couple of years but what was the point? I could still live comfortably on my pension and I had devoted a lot of time and effort to the Scottish Prison Service. It was also the chance for me to spend a lot more time with my family. That was the biggest influence on my decision. I had put a lot of hours in at Craiginches both on shifts and into their extra-curricular activities, like the fund-raisers and projects we had worked on. My family had been supportive throughout but it was time for me to give back to them and to give them my full attention. I also thought it might give me time to improve my bowling and to do a bit more gardening.

I felt I had made a positive contribution to Craiginches. I

honestly felt I couldn't top what I had done. I knew I could leave with my head held high and look back on what everyone had achieved in our time together at HMP Aberdeen with great pride.

The ironic thing was that when I finally did say farewell to the Scottish Prison Service I still wasn't back at Craiginches. I was still seconded at the training college. So my final shift with the prison service when I retired in 1996 was in Polmont. I, obviously, had to go back to Craiginches to clear my locker and to pick up my belongings but that was pretty much it. I said my goodbyes and everything was pretty low key. There was no retirement or farewell party.

The governor, Bill Rattray, gave all his departing officers a pint glass to mark our service at Craiginches. He said his thank yous and after that it was pretty much all over. Twenty odds years and suddenly it was finished.

There were, in fairness, a few of us who had retired at Craiginches at the same time. So there was also a sort of changing of the guard, with the older officers heading for the exit. It was sad to be saying farewell but I knew in my heart of hearts I had made the right decision. I also received some nice farewell cards and letters from people I had helped and got close to through the years.

This was one of them:

Dear Bryan,

On behalf of the staff and patients of Ward 19 at Woodend and myself I would like to say thank you for all the work you did fund-raising and organising social activities for all the patients through the Community Links Committee.

It involved a tremendous amount of work and effort from you and the team and it really has been much appreciated.

Best wishes from all of us for a long and happy retirement from the Scottish Prison Service.

> *Fiona Thomson*
> *City Hospital*
> *Urquhart Road*
> *Aberdeen*

It was good when you got feedback like that because, for me, my time with the Scottish Prison Service was all about helping others. I think and I hope that others feel the same about their work in the service now.

I often think back to my time at Craiginches and all the colleagues I worked alongside. I also worked under a few governors who had their own individual ways of keeping the prison and prisoners in line. Here they are:

Mr Duncan McIvor
A good governor to work for and he kept good discipline.

Mr Swanson

Mr Dan Robertson
A good governor who got a lot of respect from his staff.

Mr Mike Milne
I enjoyed working with him. He was a good governor. I also worked with him at the Scottish Prison Service College at Polmont when I was down on detached duty.

Mr Scott Oglivie
When I returned from my initial training course at Polmont I worked with him on the 2nd floor in A Hall never thinking

he would end up being my governor. It was with him that we really got started on our outside projects with the prisoners. He gave me his full backing on the projects and I enjoyed working with him.

Mr Leslie McBain

My programme with the outside projects and the visiting entertainment was in full swing by this time and he always gave the committee his full backing with what we wanted to organise. He also oversaw the centenary celebrations event at Craiginches. He was an excellent governor to work for and during his period we had the best staff training programmes in the Scottish Prison Service.

Mr William Rattray

The projects were still in full swing during this period. He also encouraged us to continue organising the Burns Suppers and Christmas parties. He would bring along his guitar and do his bit of entertaining the visitors and I enjoyed working with him. It was during his time we had a visit from the Princess Royal.

Every governor along with every member of their staff did their bit to make Craiginches the success it was. We can all look back on our time there with a great sense of pride. I am now happily retired but I would say that I am even busier now. I just don't know how I managed to fit in my day job and everything else we did when Craiginches was in its prime.

41

CRAIGINCHES NO MORE

It was announced on 8th June 2008 that Her Majesty's Prison Aberdeen was to close. It wasn't even the headline news. Okay, it maybe wasn't a surprise. Everybody who had worked and been involved at Craiginches knew this day was coming but it was buried under the announcement of a new super-jail for the north-east of Scotland.

The Scottish Prison Service had confirmed ambitious plans to build a new jail in Peterhead. It was to be called HMP Grampian and would hold around 500 inmates. It was confirmed that HMP Grampian would replace HMP Aberdeen and Peterhead. Both were to close once the new facility was up and running. HMP Grampian was also planned to be built on the existing site of HMP Peterhead so that meant there was no longer going to be a prison in Aberdeen. It had been clear that was always going to be the case. Most of the sites they had considered had been in and around Peterhead. I don't know if that was down to the fact that buying land would be cheaper than in Aberdeen or not, but it was a shame to see the city no longer having its prison.

The £90 million plans were unveiled by Mike Ewart, Chief Executive of the Scottish Prison Service.

He confirmed this in a statement, which read: 'This exercise has now been completed and we have concluded that the preferred site for HMP Grampian is on the site of the existing HMP Peterhead.

'SPS will seek planning permission from Aberdeenshire Council for the proposed development.

'Subject to receipt of planning consent, SPS will award a contract for the construction of the proposed HMP Grampian which will be run by the Scottish Prison Service.'

I remember the Scottish Government at the time had pledged to build a 'world class' facility and in fairness when you saw the plans that was to prove the case.

They certainly didn't disappoint. I was amazed when I saw everything that HMP Grampian was going to offer. There was to be accommodation for adults, females and young offenders. There were education facilities, and a community reintegration building, which was designed for helping prisoners to get ready for life after their release.

I'd had my suspicions for some time. HMP Aberdeen was becoming more and more antiquated because it was such an old building, despite all the money spent on it and the modernisation the Scottish Prison had done.

I then had read in the newspapers that the Scottish Prison Service were looking at early plans for the 'super-jail' in the North-east, before their plans for HMP Grampian were announced. I knew then the writing was pretty much on the wall for Craiginches. There was no way they were going to build a new jail and keep both the prisons in Aberdeen and Peterhead open. That was never going to happen.

Prison chiefs had also started to build these new 'super jails' around the United Kingdom and normally it meant merging one or two prisons. There is a new facility, HMP Berwyn, in Wales. The new prison has been built and as a result four

English prisons in Reading, Dorchester, Blundeston and Northallerton were all closed. In Scotland we have also seen the new HMP Addiewell Prison built in West Lothian.

The government has made it clear they are looking to build several new modern, state-of-the-art prisons. I remember reading a statement from the then Chancellor George Osborne recently about prison modernisation. It read: 'This spending review is about reform as much as it is about making savings.

'One important step will be to modernise the prison estate. So many of our jails are relics from Victorian times on prime real estate in our inner cities.

'So we are going to reform the infrastructure of our prison system, building new institutions which are modern, suitable and rehabilitative. And we will close old, outdated prisons in city centres, and sell the sites to build thousands of much-needed new homes.' The preference was always to build new modern facilities that I suppose to an extent were more prisoner-friendly. In fairness the new super-jail at Peterhead was one of the first of its time. I knew once they had the plans drawn up and were given the green light for the funding of the build then Craiginches was always going to be on borrowed time.

However, I have to admit to being disappointed when I first heard the news. I had spent a large chunk of my life there, albeit on the right side of the bars. I had made so many friends, had such good times and more importantly had done so many positive things in the name of HM Prison Aberdeen that it was a blow to hear that it was to be demolished and left as nothing more than a pile of rubble.

There was opposition to the move to close Craiginches. The then MP for Aberdeen South, Anne Begg, put up a rather staunch defence. Begg, speaking in the wake of the announcement, said: 'While I am supportive of the new prison in

Peterhead, I still believe there is a need for Aberdeen to have a prison of its own in order to retain the prison place capacity and for the short-term holding of remand prisoners close to their court appearances.' Support for that particular cause continued to grow and that led to several members of the Scottish Parliament getting together to put pressure on the government to keep smaller community prisons open. It was worth the fight but I think everyone connected with Craiginches, in their heart of hearts, knew that it was a decision that was never going to be reversed.

So, personally, I was disappointed but the basic fact was that it was the right decision by the Scottish Prison Service. Craiginches was tired and dated when I retired so twenty years on I could only imagine that it had become even more antiquated. To me, Craiginches was no longer fit for purpose. It was time for the prison to be mothballed.

You always have to remember that the prison service did spend a lot of money trying to bring Craiginches into the twenty-first century but everything they did proved a costly affair. Everything was a huge, huge ask because of the age of the building and because it was such a solid building. Peterhead was along the same lines and offered similar headaches.

I saw what a huge task it was to put in the heating and toilet facilities. It was massive and it really improved the prison but were the improvements appreciated by the prisoners? I don't think they were by a lot of them.

There were also increasing problems at Craiginches long after I retired. Overcrowding was a major factor. The prison was originally designed for around 150 but at times there were more than 250 prisoners in Craiginches. I read a lot of stuff in the media about overcrowding and staff shortages.

There was also the change in society itself. Drugs had

become an even bigger problem than they ever were in my day.

I read a report back in 2009 from Andrew McLellan, the former chief inspector of the prisons, who said that a large majority of inmates could be tested positive for illegal drugs due to the flourishing narcotics trade in the prison. When you looked more closely behind the scenes then it was clear for all to see that HMP Aberdeen or Craiginches was no longer fit for purpose.

What did disappoint me were the plans for the famous old site at Craiginches.

It was a shame, to me, that the prison was to be knocked down and then affordable flats and houses built on that site. HMP Aberdeen was always an imposing, grand building. It was a landmark in Aberdeen and I just thought they could have used it and modernised it by keeping the wall and some of the frontage for modern flats, like they do now. But the decision was to demolish it and all that history was gone. I am sure some of the prisoners who served time there would have been celebrating and glad to see the back of it.

You can understand why a developer would want the site because it is 5.6 hectares and housed twelve buildings when the jail was still standing. You could build a fair number of houses on it.

It was just such a waste. Even the granite from Craiginches couldn't be reused. I remember I asked one of the workmen when they started the demolition and he told me the granite was being taken away and he had no idea if it was going to be reused.

Craiginches closed its gate for the final time in January 2014 after 124 years. Over the previous weeks Aberdeen's final prisoners, more than 200 of them, had been transferred to alternative facilities at Perth and Barlinnie.

They remained there until HMP Grampian was officially opened two months later in March 2014.

The old site remained dormant until the demolishers started work to clear Craiginches of all its history.

I made several trips down to the site to see the gradual progress that was made in the clearing operation. Myself and Ernie Christie spoke to the site foreman who told us there would, at least, be a reminder of Craiginches on the site. There is a wall going up at the front of it and the centenary brick is going into that. I think there has been some halfway house agreement, as there is going to be a frontage to the new houses and the original prison bell is going into that. At least there will always be a constant reminder of what was HMP Aberdeen, or Craiginches.

42

REUNION

I thought that with Craiginches set to be met with the wrecking ball and the demolition team it would be as good a time as any to have a prison reunion. I thought it would be a good idea to get together with some old faces and to reminisce and to remember some of the good times connected with our time together at the prison.

So I contacted Ernie Christie and Allan MacKinnon, who were also retired, but who I'd kept in touch with, to get their thoughts. They were both pretty positive about the idea and so we arranged to meet up to see if we could make it happen.

We had the meeting and the general feeling was that we should give it a go. We had a colleague, John Watt, who wanted to come and help us. John had close links with Craiginches in our glory years and so we got him involved. It was, like we always said with the Links Committee, the more hands the merrier.

We laid down our basic plans of what we hoped to do to organise the evening. It wasn't an easy project to plan and we didn't have any finances behind us. We also didn't have a record of all the staff who had worked at Craiginches or contact details for how to get in touch with them.

It was a case of trying to get word out about the reunion but we also needed to get a bit of sponsorship behind us for printing posters and tickets.

Allan and I spent a bit of time going through the options and visiting restaurants and hotels in the city to find a suitable venue. We knew we needed to find somewhere that was accessible for parking, trains, buses and whatever other means of transport our former colleagues were going to use. We eventually decided on the Balmoral suite of the Carmelite Bar & Grill in the city centre of Aberdeen as our chosen venue. The restaurant staff told us it could hold eighty people easily and we thought that was a more than reasonable figure to aim for.

We got everything organised and set up and we thought we were well on our way until our plans took a major setback. We were hit the hammer-blow news that John Watt, one of our committee, had passed away. That set us back big time. John was a close friend and it was hard for us to take in the news. He had been heavily involved in the early stages and a major driving force in things. It came as such a shock. It took a bit of time for us all to get over. We even thought about cancelling things because we weren't sure it was right to push ahead with our plans in the circumstances. We left things for a few weeks and we also had to pay our respects to John and his family. We let John's funeral pass to give his family and all his friends, myself included, time to get over his death. I remember his funeral at Aberdeen Crematorium. It was absolutely full, with people having to stand at the sides and the back. That showed how popular John was.

I canvassed the views of Ernie and Allan to see if there was still a will and a want to go ahead with the event. The general feeling was that John thought the reunion was a worthwhile event – that was why he had decided to get involved in the organising committee in the first instance. So we decided to push ahead with our plans – although John would be sadly missed.

We decided the date would be 11th April 2015 and the venue, as mentioned, the Carmelite Restaurant in Aberdeen. It was later than we had initially planned and so it really had to be full steam ahead to get everything organised and in place for the big night.

We had to get word out. We knew that was the key because we had to try and spread the word as far and wide as we could to try and get as many of Craiginches former colleagues informed as we could. We would have liked to get every single one, who was still with us, but we knew that would be near impossible, with people's lives taking different paths and ending up all over the world.

We went public with our planned date and venue via the mainstream press. The *Press and Journal* and *Evening Express* newspapers helped us and so did the local radio stations, Original 106 FM and Northsound One and Two. Even the *Sunday Post* got in touch with us to help us and to give us a bit more national publicity.

We also managed to secure a major sponsor. Kenneth Black, a successful businessman in the city, agreed to give us the financial backing we needed. We were lucky because Kenneth's dad, Bill, worked with us at the prison. He was a civilian in the works department, where his main tasks were bricklaying and slating. That allowed us to upgrade our menu, to a choice of food selections. Norma at the Carmelite was also really helpful assisting us with menus, tickets and taking care of all the small things. Tickets went quite steadily and we hit the thirty mark quite quickly. Tickets continued to go steadily and on the night more than sixty-five former colleagues plus their partners attended the reunion. Included within that number were two gentlemen retired prison officers that had been responsible for escorting Henry J. Burnett to the gallows for the final time back in 1963.

Things went really well and the night was an overwhelming success. The response we got from all who turned up was first class.

It was brilliant going round the tables, meeting old acquaintances and seeing so many smiles on people's faces. There was a real buzz about the night and it looked like everyone enjoyed it.

We also had a raffle to make money for good causes, in the usual Craiginches style and spirit. All the prizes were donated by the people who attended the reunion. We made £260 from selling tickets, with all the money going to the new Renal Unit that is in the process of being built at Stonehaven Hospital. The reason why we decided on that was the fact that Allan MacKinnon, one of the driving forces behind the evening, had gone through a successful kidney transplant when he was still working at Craiginches. We thought it was fitting that the money should go there.

The response to the raffle after the event was just as uplifting and a number of thank you cards and emails began to drop in. Here are one or two responses.

An enormous thank you to Ernie Christie, Allan MacKinnon and yourself, and the other people who helped, for arranging the reunion.

You went above and beyond the call of duty, if you pardon the pun.

But all the extras like the tiepins, menus and the huge raffle made it a really enjoyable and remarkable evening. My wife, Margaret, even commented on how great the night was.

It was amazing and I would not have missed it for anything.

People will be sorry they did not attend when they find out how truly remarkable it was.

The fact that some of the boys were in the over-eighty bracket was also great.

The night went so quickly that I was unable to talk to everyone although I had a good go at it.

I really have a lot to be thankful for between the Scottish Prison Service and the staff I have served with in Aberdeen, Shotts and Peterhead. They have helped to shape me and my future for the last thirty-five years.

Like switching the light mode OFF.

All the best for the future,

Harry and Margaret Hopkins.

*

Well, what can I say? Many congratulations and a huge thank you for organising such a wonderful occasion on Saturday. I am still reliving it and the loads of conversations we all had. It was also so sad to hear of the passing of some of our colleagues over recent years.

It was such a surreal evening and I am so proud to be part of it. My time at 'Craigie' was a really happy time, even though as in life there were bad times, and to still be friends with my female officers, it was just an amazing night.

I hope life is good and kind to you all,

Thank you so much for everything.

Jayne Reid.

*

A special message just to say thank you very much for a special evening and your company.

Isabel and Peter Smith

(Peter was a retired chief at Craiginches)

*

Just a quick note to say thank you to yourself, Ernie and Allan for a great evening.

There must have been a lot of time and effort put in behind the scenes into making it such a great night with such good food and company.

It was nice to see some of the old faces once again.

Thanks again to all involved.

From

Ally Grant

*

WOW. You must all be so proud of how well last night went. Give yourselves a huge pat on the back.

There were lots of kent faces but thank goodness for the name badges, that was a stroke of genius.

I do hope there aren't too many sore heads today but I am sure everyone who attended will have gone away with very happy memories.

It would be great if we kept in contact as I think very fondly of my time at Craigie.

Again, a huge thank you for organising the reunion.

Regards to all,

Anne Kennedy

*

Reading all the cards and messages of congratulations and seeing all the people at the reunion made all our work worthwhile. It was a lot of work for all three of us on the organising committee, but it went so well that I am delighted we decided to take the reunion on. It has also helped to reconnect a few old friendships amongst people who may have lost touch since they and Craiginches departed. That for me and everyone on the committee was job done.

43

A Little Bit About Me

I have told you my story from HMP Aberdeen but my formative years were spent in the village of Insch in Aberdeenshire. I was the only son to Eddie and Janet Glennie.

I wasn't in my new home that long because we were soon on the move. But it wasn't a big upheaval. We were only going three doors up, as the Glennie family moved to 5 Church Terrace. It was a very lively household, thanks pretty much to my three older sisters, Madeleine, Elma and Elsie.

I had a very happy childhood with a lot of my time spent in the great outdoors. I have fond memories of bus trips to Aikey Brae fair and my regular visits to Tarlair swimming pool with the local Sunday School.

It was perfect for the great outdoors because we were very fortunate to have Bennachie close by. I have climbed that hill many times and will always remember the day we climbed it at four o'clock one clear morning, along with a couple of friends, to see the sun rise over Banff. What a sight it was and well worth the early start.

We also had Dunnydeer Castle hill, where we did our sledging in the winter, and on a nice day you also had a beautiful view from the top.

My mum used to work in the kitchen at our local school, Insch Junior Secondary School. Unfortunately, I lost my dad when I was twelve years old and my mum when I was twenty-six. It was hard for her bringing up four children, but I will always be proud of the start in life she gave me and to all my sisters. She did everything for us and I never wanted for anything.

Church Terrace was a super place to be brought up. We had lovely neighbours and it was a really friendly place. We, ironically, lived next door to a family who were also called Glennie but we were not related. It was in the terrace, along with the other Glennie boys, that I started to play football. We spent half our time having to sneak into gardens to rescue our ball back but it helped us hone our skills.

I recently returned to Insch to visit my old street and you could hardly get room to do a three-point turn never mind play football, but I suppose that would be the same in most streets now we are in the twenty-first century and most people have cars. Street football has also become a thing of the past.

Also beside us we had Granny Gibson, who I mentioned earlier, but she is worth a second mention – a wonderful lady who used to wash the football kit for our local Insch team. I would pick up the big brown case filled with the clean kit and then take the dirty one back at night for her to wash again ready for the next game.

Managers these days might have their own noticeboards but for the Insch FC team we had to go to the local butcher's to see if we were for the chop. The team line-up was normally put in his window for the next game.

I also started to support Aberdeen Football Club. They were our local senior team. I used to regularly go and watch the Dandy Dons. It was a bit of a trek but it was a small price to pay to see my Aberdeen heroes – Archie Glen, Paddy Buckley and Graham Leggat – in action. I used to take the train from Insch to Kittybrewster station, which has since disappeared, and then I would walk over Froghall to Pittodrie with a neighbour of mine, Thelma Smith, who is still a Dons supporter and still lives in Insch.

Thelma Smith went on to become matron at the local Insch War Memorial Hospital.

I enjoyed my education at Insch Junior Secondary School and in my early years I was lucky to have the two Miss Forbes, who were both lovely ladies. I was heavily involved in sport at school. I was the captain of Dunnydeer Sports Team and I was also the sports champion, along with Evelyn McWilliam, who was the girls champion. I also played for the school football team and was even lucky enough to be picked to play for the Donside and District Select. We played against a Dundee select, although we got beaten 1–0.

I was very much into technical subjects at school and went into Aberdeen to serve my time as a lathe turner at Barry Henry & Cook. I stayed in digs with a lovely couple, Mr and Mrs Black, above the Rose Bowl pub in Hutcheon Street. They were like a second mum and dad to me. I thought I was safe enough staying with the Blacks although I had to be evacuated from their flat twice. It had nothing to do with them or their cooking as the nearby comb works went on fire on two separate occasions.

I will always remember an interview for a job I had with a gentleman called Mr Watson. I was trying to get a job as an apprentice engineer at Barry Henry & Cook. I sat down and within minutes he asked which football team I played for. At that point I was playing for Inverurie Loco Works A team. That was as far as the interview went. He then told me to start a week on Monday. I was just lucky to be playing for Loco Works A at that time because we had an excellent works team with Highland league and Junior league players.

After I served my time I came home to Insch to be a postman. It was a special time in my life being a country postie. We were so important to the community. We were not only delivering their mail but also their messages from the local shop and their prescriptions from the local chemist. We were like the village messenger in some of the more remote places. By this time I had met my wonderful wife Hazel at the local dance hall and got married and we have been together now for fifty-three wonderful years. We have also been blessed with two lovely daughters, Jacqueline and Lesley, and three smashing grandchildren, Jordon, Greg and Jason.

I also started to teach keep-fit classes for the local footballers and also started playing for Insch FC. We had a very successful team, winning many trophies, including the season we won the champions cup beating all the top teams from the Aberdeenshire leagues. I also started working with an old schoolteacher friend of mine, Gordon Gerrie, in the local boxing club, where we ran a very successful club with many district champions and one Scottish champion Harry Johnstone.

While involved with the boxing I passed all my exams and became a Scottish Amateur Boxing Association judge and referee. As you know those were qualifications I went on to more than use throughout the years.

I was pretty active within the Insch community. I became a church officer at our local parish church, working with the Reverend Rodney McDonald. I had a great relationship with him. My main duties were looking after the church, the grounds and the church hall. I also had to look after the clock in the steeple, which needed a lot of tender loving care.

When the Post Office strike was going on I felt I needed a change of direction, as I had a young family who needed a more secure future. I had several discussions with the reverend about my career possibilities. He was always very positive about my future and urged me to look for a fresh outlook. He helped me look at the bigger picture when my own concern was where my next pay cheque was going to come from. It was also during this part of my career that I qualified as a Scottish Football Association referee. Also, as you now know, I decided to join the Scottish Prison Service and the details of my career are all in the book.

I, however, did not completely sever connections with my home in Insch. I commuted for the first year from Insch until I got a house in Aberdeen. A friend and colleague of mine, Jim Lawie, is someone I will be forever grateful to, as he changed his day off that week to help me and my family move everything into Aberdeen. That move changed our lives forever and it is fair to say we have never looked back – although I will never forget my home and friends in Insch. The same goes for Craiginches and all the people I worked with and came across in my time at HMP Aberdeen, Craiginches, or 'Craigie' as we more affectionately knew it.

REST IN PEACE 'Craigie' 1891 to 2014